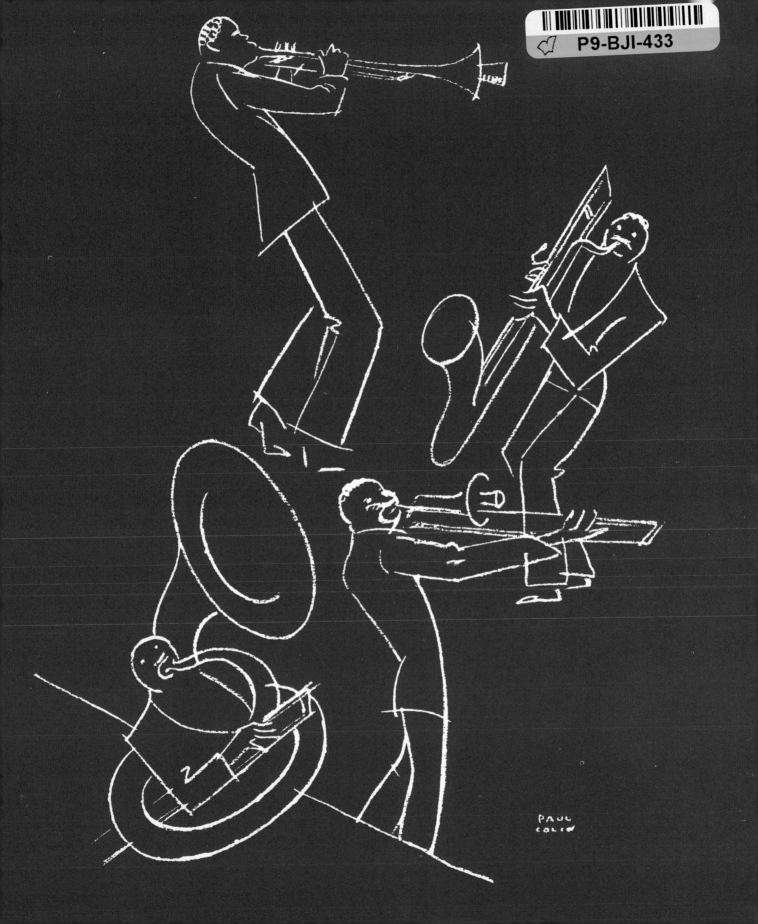

PAUL
COLIN

LES FOLIES DU MUSIC-HALL

FOR JOSÉPHINE BAKER

LES FOLIES DU MUSIC-HALL

A HISTORY OF THE MUSIC-HALL IN PARIS FROM 1914 TO THE PRESENT DAY

JACQUES DAMASE

WITH A FOREWORD BY NOËL COWARD

SPRING BOOKS
LONDON · NEW YORK · SYDNEY · TORONTO

Contents

© 1960 by Editions 'Spectacles' Paris
Translation © 1962 Anthony Blond Ltd.
First published in Great Britain 1962
by Anthony Blond Ltd

This edition published 1970 by
The Hamlyn Publishing Group Ltd
London · New York · Sydney · Toronto
Hamlyn House, Feltham, Middlesex, England

Printed in Hong Kong by
Lee Fung Printing Company Limited

SBN 600 35410 5

Foreword

W<small>HEN</small> I <small>WAS</small> a little boy I was lucky enough to be taken to the Theatre quite
often. Occasionally the outing would be to a Music Hall instead, and this I loved;
there was an excitement about the evening from the noisy, brassy overture
onwards. I found it thrilling to watch the numbers of the turns change on the
illuminated plaques at both sides of the proscenium, each one filling me with fresh
anticipation. Then, at the age of eleven I 'went on the Halls' myself in a sketch called
'A Little Fowl Play' with Sir Charles Hawtrey, and when I was thirteen in a sketch
called 'War In The Air'. In the latter I played a child with a one-track mind who
prayed each night in the prologue, 'Please God make me a great big aviator one day'
This prayer was answered in a flash, at the beginning of the very next scene to be
precise, when I (suddenly grown up and remarkably changed in looks, even to
the colour of my eyes) stepped into an aeroplane and whizzed off on a wire round
the edge of the Dress Circle, or rather half way round where, on the first night,
the whole contraption stuck and the effect was thenceforward abandoned.

With these two sketches I played in most of the London Variety houses, from the
Palladium and the Coliseum to the Willesden Hippodrome and the Shoreditch
Empire, and I adored every minute. I got to the theatre as early as I possibly
could and was usually made up and ready before the overture, so that I could stand
at the side and watch the other turns. In this way I saw Nellie Wallace, Maidie Scott,
Phil Ray, George Robey, Beattie and Babs, all the great ones in fact, from that
special and visually beautiful angle, the wings. I shall never forget them, each
turn had for me its special fascination – the performing dogs, the performing seals,
the stars who 'topped the bill', the snake charmers (I let a whole basket of snakes
loose between the matinée and evening performances one wicked day, to the
consternation of Madame Alicia Adelaide Needham and her Ladies Choir) and I
learnt a great deal.

When I was twenty I went to Paris for the first time, fell in love with it as young
people usually do and I have remained in love with it ever since. Mistinguett and
Maurice Chevalier were appearing in a revue at the Casino de Paris and of course
I went to see them. I hadn't much French but what little I had I was extremely
proud of, and that very day I had conducted the purchase of a tie with great
fluency and flair. (The friend I was with was deeply impressed; until the end of the
transaction that is, when to the saleswoman's final *Bonjour Monsieur* and to her
great surprise and my mortification, I replied before I could stop myself, *Aujourd'hui*
with a slight bow from the waist and sickening clarity.)

But my lack of knowledge of *argot* hardly mattered while watching two
individual performers as great as Mistinguett and Chevalier. I had by this time seen
many of the French stars in London where they had been enjoying a tremendous
vogue and much adoration – Gaby Deslys, drenched in pink ostrich feathers,
Alice Delysia and Morton at the Ambassadors, Regine Flory at the Palace, Yvonne

Arnaud who up till then had been appearing in musical comedies, and Raquel Meller proffering her violets and her vast eyes to the Coliseum audiences.

So I was not altogether unprepared for the shock of seeing the Paris Music Hall for the first time. I already had some idea of the power the French performers injected into their sad love songs, the hilarious low humour into the funny ones, their finesse in the witty ones and above all I had been bowled over by their glamour and the strength of their personalities.

But of all the assaults on the senses made by the Music Hall, the visual impact is for me the most memorable. One after another, quick and fast, the pictures were created; unforgettable, painted on the brain for ever. Most of them sharp, unsubtle, in the primary colours; some of them, in the *café-concerts* and the theatres where smoking was allowed, softened and a little blurred. Through the gauze curtain woven by the smoke from many cigarettes one saw the line of high-kicking girls, glittering in their sequinned *maillots*. Or through the shaft of light thrown on to the touching picture of Mistinguett in her rags, singing 'J'en ai marre', the smoke from one cigarette would curl upwards in a spiral; given momentary form, a white solidarity almost, as it hit the spotlight, only to vanish in the darkness above it, or be blown into the auditorium by some resin scented draught from the stage.

Toulouse Lautrec captured all this with paper and chalks, as Sickett captured it for us in England with oils and canvas. In this book it has all been caught by the camera – the singers, the dancers, clowns, acrobats, tight-rope walkers, jugglers, contortionists and trick cyclists; the light, the feathers, *les nus* and the spangles. It seems to me that these photographs give us the pictorial essence of the subjects they set out to portray. For those of us who never saw Damia, for instance, here she is with her chalk-white face and her tight black dress; Dranem, Jenny Golder and Mayol exactly, I am sure, as their public knew and loved them. The ones we shall never see again, Grock, Little Tich, Harry Pilcer and Barbette, are brought back to us vividly as we remember them. And the stars of today, Piaf, Joséphine Baker, Chevalier, Yves Montand, Marlene Dietrich, Charles Trenet, Suzy Solidor, Juliette Greco, they too are here to remind us of the pleasure they have given us and, more important, the promise of further pleasure to come.

1914-1918: From Café-Concert to Music-Hall

The Concert–Damia.

THE GREAT WAR was at its height, Mata–Hari was about to be shot and the Paris taxis were loading up for the Marne . . .

Damia, already a name, had her own part to play in the events of the time: she was directing and starring in the Concert–Damia.

Every day and every performance had its own individual character. On matinée days, the house was packed with rows of young scented and uniformed dandies, the local 'girls' squeezed in beside them. At about five o'clock the girls would go off to have their hair done because, in the large music-halls, crammed with troops of all nations, the angelus ringing at six was the signal for the promenade to open. Other women, in relaxed couples, unencumbered by men, would rest their pallid faces on the edges of boxes: here and there a sickly face, pitted and eaten away by cocaine . . .

Then *she* would make her entrance . . .

With the back of her hand, she would brush away the dense clouds of smoke that hung about the stage. All the drug-addicts of Montmartre would be there. Like Rollinat, Damia attracted neurotics. She never stinted herself, she showered them with blood, singing Jules Jouy's *Veuve*:

Car ses amis claquant du bec
Dès la première épreuve
Ne couchent qu'une fois avec la Veuve . . .

7

The swish of the guillotine . . . Her hand would nonchalantly mime the action. And her audience of lost boys, who were vainly trying to forget the war, would be brought back to it with a jolt – the war which only a few hundred miles away was pursuing its bloody course by land, sea and in the air . . . Then Damia would announce *La Chasse*. Extending her lovely arms towards the battlefields, she would break into the song:

> *Hurlant près des bois des corbeaux*
> *Dont les arbres sont des flambeaux,*
> *Les loups profanent des tombes,*
> *Les loups de Prusse et de Lusace.*
> *Mais une voix s'écrie: Assez!*
> *Le grand veneur des temps passés,*
> *Les vivants et les trépassés*
> *Se levent pour la Grande Chasse . . .*

Her audience of prostitutes and neurotics of both sexes would shudder. On stage, a diabolical smile would fade from Damia's lips. Like some crazed rioter, her head flung back, her dark amber eyes drinking in the red of the spotlights, she would remind the girls, in the tinselly words of the song, that the law of Zarathustra still held good: man is for war; woman for the recreation of the warrior.

Damia, in her tight black velvet sheath of a dress, her arms flailing the air, tossing back her dark-gold hair with a flick of her head, created a goddess of pleasure that has probably never been seen in real life.

Most of the audience were French troops. There were a few men in evening dress and pearl-necklaced women sitting in boxes. Anyone who'd done well out of the war would go and see Damia, it was the smart thing.

One night, the Concert-Damia had to close down. Big Bertha was booming. German planes were raining down showers of bombs on Paris. The gas-works at Vincennes blew up. Damia went back to appearing in local *café-concerts*.

Three highly original performers came to the fore during this period: Damia, Yvonne George, and Fréhel. They simply brought their own lives to the footlights. All knew the cost of the struggle, the meaning of poverty and how artists used drugs in a hopeless attempt to achieve the impossible: oblivion. Utrillo and Modigliani drank: they drugged themselves.

Gaby Deslys arrives with the jazz-band.

> *Y a du jazz-band partout, le jour et la nuit,*
> *Y a du jazz-band partout, bonjour Paris,*
> *Y a du jazz-band,*
> *Y a du jazz-band,*
> *Y a du jazz-band partout,*
> *Y a des jazz-band qui rendent les hommes fous . . .*

While Damia, Yvonne George and Fréhel exploited the wretchedness
of their lives, Gaby Deslys returned to France with a golden legend
of royal amours, prodigious wealth – and jazz. A native of Marseilles, she
brought back from New York millions of jewels – a living embodiment
of the new-style Music-Hall in both Old and New Worlds. Her
brown hair dyed a conventional blonde, her Marseilles accent sprinkled
with English intonations – a new snobbery – she was heralded by a
fanfare of publicity. A minor king, Manuel of Portugal, had staked his
throne on her looks, Yankee millionaires had strewn their riches
at her feet, though every night she played in New York she earned a
fortune.

Gaby Deslys had been less struck by her fabulous millionaires
than by her discovery of a splendid, tall, dark, young man who
danced as naturally as most people breathe – and with tremendous style.
This young American of Hungarian descent played an important
part both in her career and her affections. Together, they became the most
celebrated couple ever to appear on the music-hall stage. His name
was Harry Pilcer. She also brought back several of her successful
New York numbers and, that February, the Folies-Marigny won her from
competing music-halls at a cost of 200,000 francs which was, at
that time, an enormous salary for Paris.

Gaby Deslys also introduced the jazz-band to Paris. Its instruments
ranged from saxophones to revolver shots. And for the first time
a music-hall actress appeared on stage, smothered in plumes and feathers,
bejewelled like a queen, performing dances 'of an almost insane ferocity'.

American police, armed with revolvers, used to stand guard
over mixed white and coloured audiences, in case the onslaught of jazz
stampeded them into violence. The tone of modern Music-Hall was
set and many people welcomed it as a long-awaited release
from the old theatrical conventions.

9

Neurosis in the Music-Hall: Yvonne George.

> *Moulin-Rouge, Moulin-Rouge,*
> *Pour qui mouds-tu, Moulin-Rouge?*
> *Pour la mort ou pour l'amour? . . .*

A native of Montparnasse, Yvonne George was, according
to her contemporaries, the greatest singer to appear after Yvette Guilbert
and the hey-day of Montparnasse.

Tall and thin, like a kind of red-haired Pierrot, with a pale face,
restless eyes and a purple gash of a mouth, she saw music-hall and
night-club audiences being fobbed off with crude re-hashes of sea-songs.
So she got rid of the chocolate-box sailors à la Théodore Botrel and
launched a new and saltier fashion.

Like Damia and Fréhel, Yvonne George never spared herself.
Each season she became more frail, the prey both of excessive drug-
addiction and harsh antidotes to drunkenness – a remedy often worse than
the disease – and she developed a passion for Montparnasse cabarets
and their new exotic atmosphere.

She loved ports: Antwerp, Marseilles and Villefranche,
American sailors coming ashore, their athletic bodies and lithe hips in
tight jerseys and bell-bottom trousers.

Yvonne George made her final appearance at Le Grand-Ecart, a
Montmartre night-club opened by Moyses. This show, organized by
Jean Cocteau, must have hastened her end. Paris society
paid five hundred francs a bottle of champagne to hear her
cracked voice for the last time, and watch her go through agony
in pathetic and hopeless attempts to move about the stage . . .

Shortly afterwards, she entered a Swiss sanatorium. The papers
announced her death, but it was a false alarm. She had
merely run away from her doctors to go and kill herself in a
port. She passed away in a hotel in Genoa, lured by the docks and the
wailing of ships' hooters.

Regine Flory

The Théâtre Mogador was modelled for Regine Flory after the style
of English music-halls. She opened with an extremely lavish
revue. She appeared on stage like a black swan, solemn and thoughtful,
twisting herself into tremorous shapes and finally dying . . .

Whenever things went wrong, she used to go back to the Cigale, her
lucky theatre, where she had her first success.

She put a bullet into her heart in a famous manager's office in London.

Jenny Golder.

Jenny Golder was a star who killed herself, apparently, because of an unhappy love-affair. Like the Dolly Sisters, she came from the United States. She began almost as a walk-on in a show with Mistinguett. She only had a few words to sing, 'but when the curtain came down on the first night of the revue,' wrote Henri Jeanson, 'Jenny Golder was famous.'

Then she became the star of a Folies-Bergère revue: 'a very attractive girl with a trick of rolling her eyes, eyes which magically dwarf the rest of her face.' She disdained gracefulness. In a comic voice, she sang

Jenny, Jenny.

For a whole winter, Paris went round squinting and humming '*Jenny, Jenny . . .*'

Then Jenny Golder starred in every music-hall in Europe.

'Jenny Golder burns up the stage,' wrote Louis-Léon Martin. 'For high-kicks, knocking out a few dance-steps, winking, juggling and making play with her fan, putting over a joke and even just showing-off a bit, Jenny Golder is unrivalled. She seems to attract the blaze of the spotlights . . .'

A few months later, disenchanted by her art, and face to face with grim realities, she lost her head and, like Régine Flory, shot herself.

11

Jane Marnac.

Another star, who approached Mistinguett in popularity, though she never had the same tremendous impact, was Jane Marnac.

The greatest performers, whether in the theatre, like Sarah Bernhardt, Jeanne Granier or Réjane, or in the Music-Hall, like Mistinguett, all had a professional authority, a disdain of sexual innuendo and feminine wiles; they possessed a kind of perfect formula for charm which had nothing to do with being women.

Jane Marnac, on the contrary, wooed her audience with a whole range of mischievous little tricks and affectations: tomboy gestures, comic intonations, sly smiles, conspiratorial winks, exploiting her peaches-and-cream looks and her supple, undulating body . . .

When she gave up acting in comedy, she headed the bill at the Casino de Paris. She had two particular successes in plays: in *L'Ecole des Cocottes* at the Variétés, and in *Manon*, by Henri Bataille and Albert Flament, at the Madeleine, in which she was outstanding.

There is a Jane Marnac style in the Music-Hall which combines both these elements, Manon and Cocotte, the witty and the soulful . . .

MATA-HARI. 1916.

MOULIN ROUGE. 1917.

DAMIA.

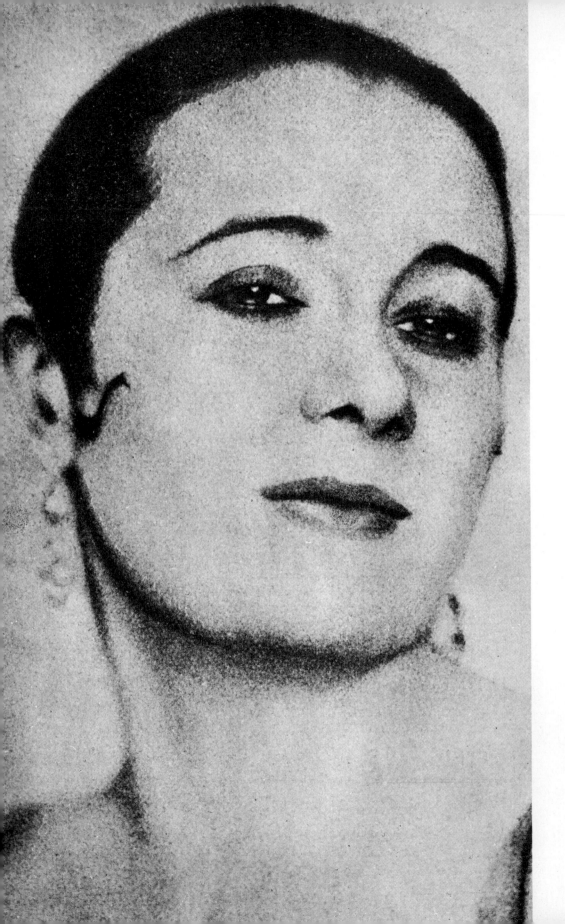

YVONNE GEORGE. 1925.

FRÉHEL.

GABY DESLYS.

GABY DESLYS. 1918.

P. 20-21. HOFFMANN GIRLS. 1924.

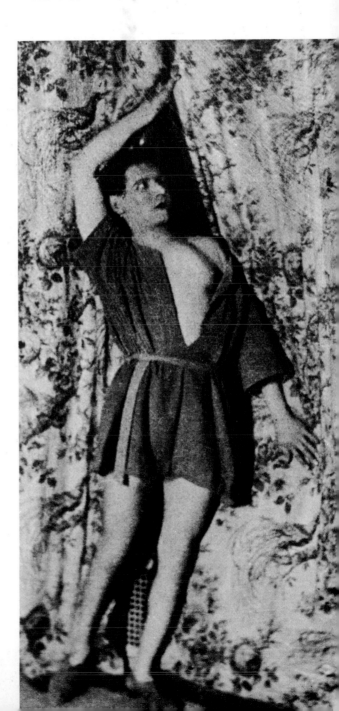

JENNY GOLDER.

JENNY GOLDER.
HARRY PILCER.

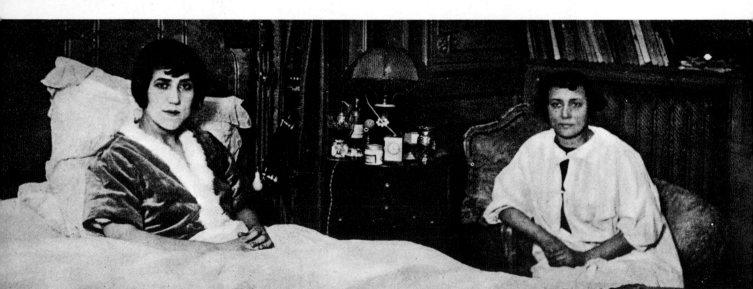

JANE MARNAC.

Mistinguett, Maurice Chevalier and Joséphine Baker

'Miss'.

MISTINGUETT AND MAURICE CHEVALIER dominate the history of
French Music-Hall. Mistinguett, made famous throughout the
world by the *valse chaloupée*, was already a big star in 1918. Chevalier, too,
had attracted attention before the war, at the Folies-Bergère. When he
returned from being a prisoner-of-war, his personality developed and his
success became so great that he threatened to dwarf 'Miss' herself. He then
left the Casino de Paris and went to the Palace Theatre, London.

All Paris adored 'Miss'. To them she was like a national
monument, which would endure for ever. But Mistinguett is dead. She
was affected by a tumour of the brain on Christmas Eve 1955, then by a
double congestion of the lung, and lay on a satin bed, wearing a pink
nightdress, surrounded by bouquets of violets and azaleas. Some
twelve days later she died in her sleep.

'Miss' – her real name was Jeanne Bourgeois – was born on the
5th April 1875 at Pointe-Raguet, near Montmorency. Her father was a
mattress-maker and her mother dressed feathers, but 'Miss' was
never anything but a music-hall artist. She was much more than that,
though: with her wit, her *faubourg* accent, her mischievous looks and
malicious tongue, her perfect legs, for sixty years she symbolized Paris, a
Paris of poets and *midinettes*, not only to foreigners, but what was
rarer, to the people of Paris themselves.

Mistinguett's success defies analysis. It was miraculous. Her career
spanned half a century. When she gave her first performance, in 1893,
she was called 'La Môme Flora': in her final appearance, at the
A.B.C. in 1950, at the age of seventy-five, she danced bebop every night for
twelve minutes non-stop. A distinguished critic wrote:

'Mistinguett lived only for her career. Nothing else really
interested her. She used to hang about impatiently until it was time to go to
her dressing-room. She learnt nothing, everything came from within.
She was a force of nature. She never developed her art, she never
tried to, quite content to remain Mistinguett, with feathers on her head, or
rags on her back, walking up and down vast staircases in her own
inimitable way, showing off her legs sheathed in silk stockings right
up to her hips – unless, of course, she happened to be wearing a pair
of old shoes with trodden-down heels.

Funny or wistful, she could make herself look either shabby or beautiful through sheer will-power. She was so sincere in her many and various parts, that at seventy she could still play a little flower-girl of sixteen without seeming ridiculous. She was so convinced herself that she was the poor child that she was able to convince her audiences.'

For many years, she was a great influence in the development of the Music-Hall in Paris. She was the only French woman star who could walk down a staircase carrying fifteen pounds of plumes on her head and dragging seven yards of feathers behind her. She was a lithe acrobatic dancer and had a flair for style, décor and production. In fact, she did much to create shows in which she was billed only as a performer. Her life was made up of hard work, precision and devotion to her art. The songs she introduced, from *J'en ai marre* to *Mon homme* and *Valencia*, have been sung the world over.

Every evening, 'Miss' had eleven changes of costume and character – from shop-girl to street-walker to fairy queen – wearing huge sprays of feathers on her head, dragging a five-yard train behind her yet gliding like a swan.

When she made her entrance, the first thing you saw was her face, and a smile, a huge smile. Her eyes would gleam in the bright lights, but the smile still hovered on her lips, the determined smile of a hostess at a party. Smiles to left and right. 'Miss', immediately sensing 'the boys' on the prompt side weren't 'with it', would wink imperiously at the culprits, but carry on distributing smiles. She would flaunt her 'nice girl' personality, her immense cheerfulness, weighing up her audience as she went; no swagger, except when she walked her consciously young, tripping walk. As she reached the footlights, she would start to sing, seeming to improvise.

That, in a nutshell, was the secret of 'Miss', the undisputed queen of Music-Hall, the true originator of the Spectacular Revue. Against patterns woven by the sinuous legs of young English chorus-girls, Mistinguett had to tell the story behind the picture, with the simple gaiety and quick-fire repartee of the streets. In spite of those cold, spiritually void settings and huge impersonal companies, she always retained her femininity. So much depended on it, particularly the forty or fifty thousand francs that had to be taken every night at the box office.

26

Maurice Chevalier.

'Character' singer, born on the 12th September 1888 in Menilmontant, son of a house-painter. His mother, whom he affectionately called '*La Louque*', was a braid-trimmer. At various times he was employed as an apprentice metal-engraver, carpenter, electrician and printer, and he made his first appearance at the Café des Trois-Lions for the price of a cup of coffee. But his first big chance came at the Casino des Tourelles when he was thirteen, for twelve francs a week . . .

At thirteen, he was a child prodigy: now, at seventy, he is a miracle of vitality. A tireless globe-trotter, he has made many films in America, among them: *Ariane* and *Gigi*. He still sings in New York, Puerto Rico and Australia. A professional charmer, he married Yvonne Vallée when he was thirty-six. At forty-seven, he fell head-over-heels in love with Nita Raya, who was then twenty. Apart from Mistinguett, she was probably the woman he loved best, though at sixty he fell for Jacqueline Noël and, at sixty-two, discovered Patachou and became a close friend of the family . . .

As soon as he walks on stage, wearing or carrying his famous straw hat, Chevalier seems to come alive. He enters with a long, measured stride – no gimmicks. His way of walking is unique. Then he starts to sing. Chevalier doesn't sing particularly well, but he has his own style which he uses to great effect, especially in comic numbers. He can't dance particularly well, either, though he has the suppleness and precision of a professional boxer.

always get a laugh from his audience by some unexpected gesture or carry off a poor song by introducing surprise effects.

How many times he must have sung:

> *Elle avait de tous petits petons*
> *Valentine, Valentine . . .*
> *Elle avait de tous petits petons*
> *Que je tâtais à tâtons . . .*

How did Mistinguett and Chevalier acquire their magnetic charm? Maurice has often told the story of his early days as a mechanic in the outskirts of Paris. Mistinguett, as a small girl, used to sing in the streets of Enghien, pushing round a cart-load of mattresses for her mother to re-stuff. The conscientiousness, the firm, inventive authority, the touches of elegance and taste, the polish of a Chevalier or a Mistinguett, derived from their knowledge of the life of the streets and of the common people, made them into supreme international entertainers.

Joséphine Baker.

This is how Joséphine Baker was described in *Candide* in an article on the *Revue Nègre*:

'Much has already been written about her. People have gone back to see her a second, even a sixth time. Others have left their seats after two numbers, stumped out of the theatre, slamming the doors and calling it a disgrace, madness, anarchy and pandering to the baser instincts . . . The revue begins at ten-fifteen . . . Paris Society crowds the darkened auditorium . . . The negro musicians file past the pearl-grey curtains with their instruments . . . The curtain rises: the scene is a port by night. Away in the distance, you can see cargo-boats lit up, the moon, bales on wharves, and women in shirts and dresses, some wearing turbans, come on stage and sing a

28

short song. All the girls seem to be negresses, except one who is white all over . . . They dance a Charleston . . . Then a curious figure dashes on stage, sagging at the knees, wearing a pair of tattered shorts and looking like a cross between a boxing kangaroo, a piece of chewing-gum and a racing cyclist – it's Joséphine Baker!'

The *Revue Nègre* was, in a sense, as revolutionary as the *Ballet Russe*, and, like it, was a subject of violent controversy, provoking extremes of enthusiasm and hatred. But it finally caught on and became a hit. In 1926, Joséphine Baker appeared for the first time at the Folies-Bergère after her triumph in the *Revue Nègre* at the Théâtre des Champs-Elysées. In 1927, she headed the bill in *Un vent de folie*. Thirty years after the *Revue Nègre*, she was dancing on a drum. Ever since the 22nd September 1925, her first appearance in Paris, with the troupe of Blackbirds, she has gone from strength to strength. She not only had engagements with Varna and Derval, she also had her own night club. She made her first 'talkie' in 1935 with Jean Gabin – *Zouzou*.

In 1940, she joined the French Women's Army. From 1940 to 1945, still in the army, she worked in London and North Africa. Born in St Louis in 1906, she has always helped and defended coloured peoples. In 1947, she married Jo Bouillon, the conductor, who toured the world with her. She then bought a property in Milandes so she could house and feed the orphaned children she had collected during the course of her travels.

She said good-bye to her Paris public in the spring of 1956. But the difficulties she ran into and the need a woman of her kind feels to appear on stage made her return to the Olympia in the autumn of 1959 in a Spectacular Revue. Even more attractive than in 1956, she succeeded in being unforgettably young, beautiful, vital, commanding and perfect. The twilight of this goddess is, as Robert Beauvais said, 'like a magnificent sunset'. Her:

> *Paris, mes amours,*
> *Il n'y a rien à faire,*
> *On y revient toujours . . .*

will be remembered as long as her *Petite Tonkinoise* or her *J'ai deux amours, mon pays et Paris* – two of her greatest triumphs . . .

29

The Magic of the Circus

Barbette, the man–woman.

JUST ANOTHER DRESSING-ROOM: perfume, a pile of silk stockings, feathers, plumes, stage jewellery and, hanging on strings from wall to wall, silver trains, gold lace and suits of spangled armour . . .

Here, in this dressing-room, the man-woman is busy completing his disguise. He does his make-up, retouches it, his dresser, his own private dresser pulls on his precious silk stockings for him, and he crams his man's skull into an incredibly blonde wig that looks as if it had been stolen from Ophelia or plundered from Gaby Deslys' romantic tomb . . .

Barbette was first presented by Lord Baradsford, at the Alhambra. He created another sensation in *Y a qu'à Paris* at the Casino de Paris in 1923. He was called Barbette, the enigma . . .

On stage, against black velvet curtains appeared a young woman in a silvery-gold wig topped with plumes and feathers, with a train of rich lamé and silver lace, undressing on a couch of rich oriental carpets. The woman then rose, naked except for the gems on her breast and belly, and began walking a steel tight-rope. Her eyes shaded green, like some mysterious Asiatic jewel, she walked backwards and forwards along the tight-rope, dispensed with her balancing-pole, and contorted her thin, nervous body as the entire audience held its breath . . . Then Barbette leapt down on to the stage, gave a bow, tore off her wig and revealed a bony Anglo-Saxon acrobat's head: gasps from the astonished audience, shattered by the sudden brutality of the action.

The Music-Hall has always had its female impersonators. But no one went further in the cult of sexual mystification than this young man who transformed himself into a jazz-age Botticelli. And to reward his disturbing, dreamlike perfection, the music-halls paid Barbette ten times as much as the average acrobat.

The Realm of Laughter. The Fratellinis.

Till now, clowns had only appeared in the circus. But circus acts and clowning became so much in demand at the time of Radiguet's *Bal du Comte d'Orgel*, the Boeuf-sur-le-Toit and *Les Six*, that theatre managers were anxious to book performers like the Fratellinis,

Grock, Porto, Pichel and many others, who slightly modified acts which had been designed for the circus arena, and added a new music-hall attraction.

One afternoon, the classical actors at the Comédie-Française gathered to receive the Fratellinis. The three clowns were welcomed in the spirit of Molière who, as a small boy, used to love watching farces acted by the Comoci Fideli. A Fratellini cult quickly sprang up. Court and society frequented their dressing-room. Princesses sent their children to see them. When the Fratellinis went off on their European tours, they dictated their own terms.

The Fratellinis and Grock dominated the realm of laughter. Albert Fratellini declared: 'We are above national differences, class differences and hierarchies, we are children involved in the quest for the wonderful and the unexpected . . .' François wore costumes covered with spangles. He was the leader of the troupe, elegant, moonstruck, with white cheeks, eyes made up to look Japanese, a dab of red on the tip of his nose, *Monsieur Clown*, the shrewd, irresistible talker . . .

Paul was *Auguste*, with a pleasant, round face, practically no make-up, a vast collar, shapeless suit and shoes like barges. *Monsieur Auguste* would seem to be a respectable citizen, but don't you believe it, he's no better than the smiling, worldly François: he too is out to humiliate the *contre-Auguste*.

The *contre-Auguste* was an original character, invented by the Fratellinis, and played with near perfection by Albert. The three brothers formed a brilliantly funny trio.

The name Fratellini still exists in show business. Anny Fratellini is a singer and François' sons are known professionally as the Craddocks.

Grock, Emperor of Clowns.

Monsieur Grock took a minute violin out of an enormous violin-case, played a few delightful variations on it and sat down at the piano. From then on, things started happening. The piano stool was set too high and too far away, so Monsieur Grock had to tug painfully at the massive grand piano to bring it closer to the stool. Then he sat down and played beautifully . . . After that, Monsieur Grock quarrelled with his partner, tore off the piano-top, slid around on it like a toboggan, sat down on the back of a chair, fell off and got up again.

Grock's voice seemed to wander about inside him. Sometimes it was in his nose, sometimes in his throat, sometimes lower down: he had all the ventriloquist's tricks at his finger-tips.

'*Pourquoâ, sans blâgue* . . .' This was the catch-phrase in his French act which he toured for several decades and brought to a pitch of rare perfection. The character he portrayed was his own double. He didn't have to act a part. He was the character, the part himself. There was Polichinelle, Arlequin and Pierrot: Now there was Grock.

Grock, passionately devoted to the profession which he entered at an early age, had been a tumbler, tight-rope walker, juggler and snake-man. Besides his remarkable talent for mime, he was a musician, acrobat, actor and author, and he could speak a dozen languages. He left his audiences convulsed with laughter. His act was the longest ever seen, either on stage or in the arena, but no one ever objected, quite the opposite . . .

This kindly Swiss, born at Reconviller in 1880, had a villa built for him in Italy: it was the most eccentric place imaginable. He eventually retired to it and died there in the summer of 1959.

Pichel and others.

A skinny little man with beady eyes and a blotchy face, his body swallowed up in a huge overcoat, an opera-hat on his head, Pichel would walk forward towards his companion, Scale, apparently oblivious of the audience. Scale was a compact, neatly-dressed man acting the part of *Monsieur Loyal*, foil to Pichel. With amiable condescension, Scale would advise Pichel to bow to the audience, and push him to the front of the stage. Without hesitating, the little man would raise his hat, revealing a great shock of hair. The audience would start laughing. From then on, Pichel would receive constant applause. Lively and petulant by turns, he communicated an inexhaustible fund of gaiety to the audience by constant arguments with the orchestra, and repeating the words: '*Je suis content*', with an odd throaty chuckle. Pichel's manner of talking was very infectious and his '*je suis content*' became as famous a catch-phrase in Paris as Grock's '*pourquoâ*'. It was impossible to forget his red braces, the way he sprang up like a monkey on to his partner's shoulders – Pichel's agility contrasting wonderfully with Scale's calm strength – his lively mimicry, his accent with its curious speech defect, his delightful way of confiding in his audience with his: '*V's avez viou?*' This gay, deformed, brilliant Goyesque caricaturist was comparable to Little Tich.

Many clowns have passed through the music-halls. Others who deserve mention include Footit, and his successors, Chocolat, Porto, Dancy, and Zavatta who was one of the finest clowns of all time.

2

1

MISTINGUETT.

1. 1903.

2. MOULIN ROUGE. 1926.

MISS ET LADD « DANS LES BOUGES LA NUIT ». 1932   1920.

MISS.

1. « TITINE ». CASINO DE PARIS. 1943.   2. BORDEAUX. 1930.

1   2

MISTINGUETT.

1. 1925.

2. MISS, FOUJITA. DEAUVILLE. 1925.

3. MISS, MAURICE CHEVALIER. 1917.

3

MAURICE CHEVALIER.

1. 1910. LA BELLE ÉPOQUE.

2. 1927.

2

MAURICE CHEVALIER. 1946.

CHEVALIER, COLETTE MARCHAND. « PLEIN FEU ». EMPIRE. 1952.

JOSÉPHINE BAKER.

CASINO DE PARIS. 1927.   « PARIS, MES AMOURS ». OLYMPIA. 1959.

1928.

1   2

JOSÉPHINE BAKER.

1. REVUE NÈGRE. 1926.

2. CASINO DE PARIS.

« PARIS, MES AMOURS ». OLYMPIA. 1959.

49

BARBETTE

VAN DER CLYDE (ALIAS BARBETTE). 1925.

DAME BARBETTE.

BARBETTE (ALIAS VAN DER CLYDE). 1925.

LES FRATELLINI.

CROCK.

55

PICHEL.   AMERICAN CLOWNS.

P. 58 PAUL COLIN : « PIERROT ». CASINO DE PARIS. 1934.

57

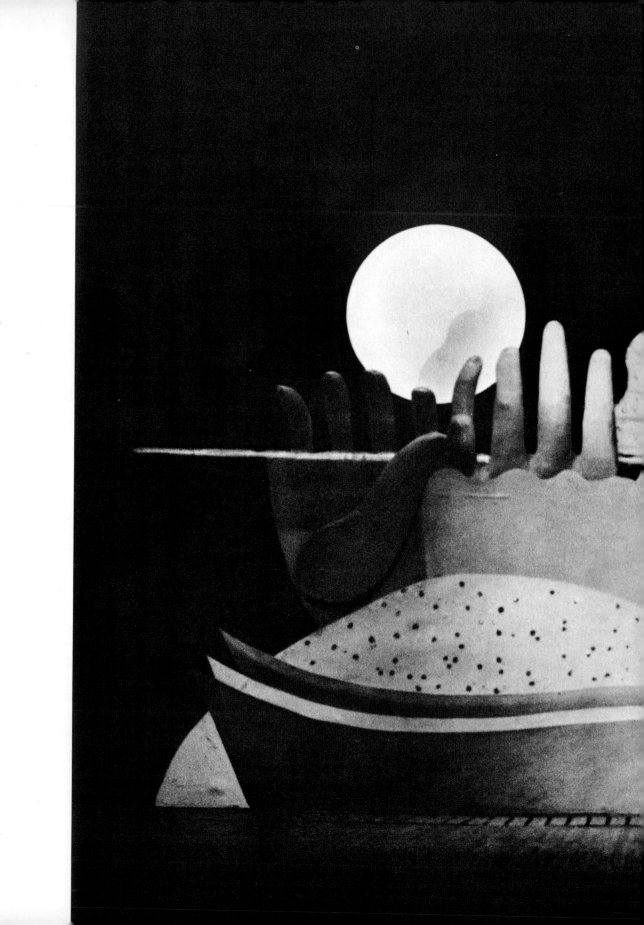

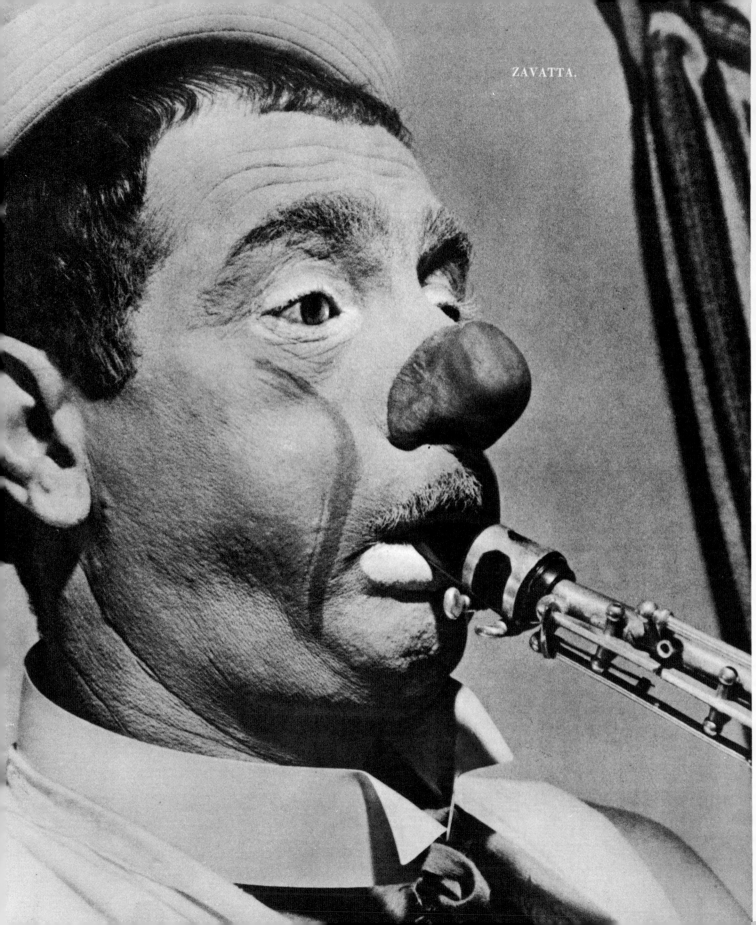

ZAVATTA.

The World of Song

From Caf' Conc' to Threepenny Opera.

THERE WERE MANY kinds of vocalist: the 'operatic' vocalist, the 'Apache', the 'dramatic', the 'swell', the 'character' vocalist, the 'eccentric', the 'comic trooper', the 'comic madman' and the 'comic drunkard'. There were no 'straight' singers, in the modern sense, relying mainly on charm. There was the Dranem type, the Polin, Mayol, Eugénie Buffet, Bordas and Valse types.

What became of them all? The talented Fortugé died young. Dranem was saved, at the end of a long career, by operetta. (What would have happened to Bourvil, the zany singer, if he hadn't broken into films and so-called musical comedy?)

Then there were the comedians who sang. One of them was called Rallum, a native of Marseilles. From the Folies-Bergère, he went to play Clemenceau at the Théâtre Marigny. One night, Marcel Pagnol was in the audience. A few months later, Rallum was no more, and in his place was Raimu, acting Pagnol's *Marius*.

And then there was Fernandel . . . He was about twenty at the time and the local hero of a Marseilles music-hall where he had already been singing for about thirteen years. Natives of Marseilles might remember having seen, in 1910, a small boy, dressed as a soldier-lad, dash on the stage of the Scala, looking rather scared. It was Fernand

Constantin, billed as Le Petit Sined, known today as Fernandel. The soldier-lad went on to sing:

> *Ah, Mademoiselle Rose,*
> *J'ai un p'tit objet à vous offrir,*
> *Ce n'est pas grand' chose*
> *Mais cela vous fera plaisir . . .*

A few years later, Fernandel was appearing in Paris at the Concert-Mayol, after which Derval engaged him as partner to Mistinguett at the Folies-Bergère. Mistinguett made her dazzling appearance, then the curtain went up on Fernandel. The scenery consisted of a plain backcloth on which was painted a huge but completely bare staircase, with three steps at the bottom, on which stood a crestfallen Fernandel, all alone, saying: 'Look at the rotten little staircase they've given me. And yet when Derval signed me up, he said: "Don't worry, you'll get just the same treatment as Mistinguett!"'

Little Yvonne Wigniole, later known throughout the world as Yvonne Printemps, made her debut at the Folies when she was about twelve or thirteen. In the 1912 revue, there was a series of tableaux featuring the châteaux of the Loire and Yvonne presented Azay-le-Rideau . . .

Jean Gabin made his debut in Moulin-Rouge revues as a chorus-boy.

Arletty was a fashion-model at Poiret's. Paul Guillaume introduced her to Berthez, director of the Capucines. She added a 'y' to Arlette to make it sound more English and up-to-date. Rip, who loved thin women, first saw her on the stage of the Capucines, singing:

> *Je m'déroule*
> *Parmi la foule,*
> *J'ai des enlacements libertins,*
> *Je suis le serpentin . . .*

Rip exclaimed: '*Mince de haricot vert!*' and immediately signed her up. For fifteen years, Arletty showed her legs in Rip's revues. For fifteen years, she played only *louche* parts. In 1934, in a revue at the Variétés, a sort of historical hotch-potch, she appeared as something out of the *bibliothèque rose:* it was a welcome change. She came on as Messalina, singing the sad chorus:

> *Je suis la femme inassouvi-i-e . . .*

Her thinness went well with her street-walker's stance – hands on hips and constantly shrugging her shoulders.

Florelle made *The Threepenny Opera* and stamped the film with her unusual personality. She made her debut at the age of twelve, in Vienna, wearing her first communion dress as a stage costume. She returned to France after 1914, sang at the Abri, the Cigale, the Capucines, and appeared with Henri Garat in the second version of *Ça c'est Paris!*

While Florelle is best remembered for her performance in *The Threepenny Opera*, Kurt Weil's music for the same film had a powerful influence at the time and his songs have been sung all over the world by Marianne Oswald, Juliette Greco, Mouloudji and, of course, Lotte Lenya. His style undoubtedly influenced Joseph Kosma and many others.

Vincent Scotto, who was born in Marseilles in 1874, and died in 1958, arrived in Paris in 1906. By then, he had already written the music of *La Tonkinoise*, for Polin. He quickly became a great success. 'Vincent, your songs will be sung in every street and home in France,' Christiné, with whom he composed many songs, told him. *Les Ponts de Paris* (1913), *Cabotin* (1916) with words by Maurice Garçon, *Mon Paris* (1925), *J'ai deux amours* (1930) which made Joséphine Baker, *Le plus beau tango du monde* (1934), *La java bleue* (1938), *Ramuntcho* (1944): these were the landmarks in the career of a man who wrote more than 4,000 songs and a dozen sensational operettas, including *Au pays du soleil* and *Violettes impériales*, which may well stay as long in the popular repertoire as *White Horse Inn* and *The Merry Widow*.

Straight singers and duettists.

By way of a change from nostalgia, wrote *Vogue* in 1934, the Bosphore presented Charpini. He would stand at the theatre entrance and pass comments on the doormen and the people going in, with a flow of rhetoric that delighted the crowds. He adored any kind of by-play or interruption. When he sang, it was impossible to tell if he was singing the real words or if they were spur-of-the-moment improvisations. At any moment, he might ask the manager to admire his voice, or go into a huddle with his pianist, or encourage his partner, Brancato, with a look, a gesture or a '*Vas-y, Mimiche*'. Together, they sang duets, such as *La Belle Hélène* or *Manon*. Charpini was the prima donna and you'd have sworn it was his real voice, had he not suddenly plunged from his top to his bottom register, producing a wonderfully sonorous bass note.

Duettists were all the rage, the popular fashion: there were Mireille, Pills and Tabet. Wiener and Doucet made Le Boeuf-sur-le-Toit famous, reading detective stories and drinking beer as they performed to audiences of artists and aristocrats. In later years, Marianne Oswald and Roger Vivier used to poke fun at Reda Claire who did, however, have some success with a series of absurd sentimental songs like *Ma banlieue* and *Ma jeunesse*. Jean Sablon murmured his way through *Je tire ma révérence* and *Vous qui passez sans me voir*, and Jean Tranchant sang *Et la servante est rousse*, *Dans le bistrot du port* and *Allez-y donc, ici l'on pêche!* . . .

*Fréhel: Le Cafard et Les Beuglants.**

Fréhel, with her forceful chin, a shrewd and resolute eye under a raised eyebrow, would plant her hands on her ample hips in the thick of the smoke-filled auditorium and prepare to crush 'some drunkard in evening-dress' with a flood of obscene repartee. Then she'd turn to her accompanist and fling a '*Vas-y, mon pote*, these ladies and gents'll soon pipe down!'

Low and husky, savage and tender by turns, her voice would soon top the uproar. 'The ferocious passion of that almost masculine face, with its fleshy cheeks and craggy outline, her aggressive laugh and cracked voice, evoked the hinterland of the Paris suburbs full of shacks, down-and-outs and street-walkers.'

Her *Grand frisé* and her *P'tit Louis*, the pimp who can't help his profession because, poor fellow, his hands are tied, and her street-walker songs, were typical Fréhel numbers. At the end of her act, she would break into that 'inevitable wail of the sirens of Montmartre': *le cafard!*

> *Non, j'suis pas saoule*
> *Malgré que je roule*
> > *Dans toutes les boîtes de nuit*
> *Cherchant l'ivresse*
> *Pour que ma tristesse*
> *Sombre à jamais dans le bruit.*
> *Je hais le plaisir qui m'use*
> *Et quand on croit que je m'amuse,*
> *J'ai des pleurs plein le coeur.*
> *J'ai l'cafard,*
> *J'ai l'cafard . . .*

* Literally: 'The Bawlers'.

And the song ended:

> *Dans ma névrose*
> *J'ai pris des tas de choses*
> *Ether, morphine et coco . . .*

Her entire audience became *Apaches*, drug-addicts, and *cafardeux*, and Fréhel was greeted with a storm of applause which must have reminded her of the local *salles de beuglants** where she returned in triumph some years ago.

Marianne Oswald's battles and the German influence.

1934 began on a note of frenzy, uproar and rebellion. Almost every evening, pro-royalist students and groups of ex-servicemen demonstrated in the streets of Paris against the inefficiency and corruption of the government. Sometimes they even ripped out the iron railings round the trees on the main boulevards and clashed with the police. Eventually, on the 6th February, shots were fired in the Place de la Concorde.

In another district of Paris, in Montparnasse, haunt of artists and foreign visitors, a different battle was being fought every night, at the time when the lights came on in the music-halls. Admirers and detractors of a new singer, making her first appearance on the stage of the Gaîté, confronted each other, hurling abuse and often coming to blows. After singing in various night-clubs, Marianne Oswald was engaged at Le Boeuf-sur-le-Toit, where she immediately became the darling of the 'regulars', the literary and artistic avant-garde, which included the leaders of the new young school of music. Milhaud and Honegger not only composed for her, they accompanied her at the piano. Max Jacob called her 'the poets' sister' and she sang Prévert's early songs. Jean Cocteau wrote *Anna La Bonne* and *La Dame de Monte-Carlo* for her. She spent the war in America. When she returned, she didn't want to sing again, preferring to entertain and broadcast to children.

'Songs of soot and flame,' wrote Albert Camus, 'that Marianne Oswald's awesome voice has sung to unhappy and anxious crowds throughout the years: a voice, full of despair, yet hopeful, because from the torrents of molten lava rises a clear and innocent spring.'

* Literally: 'bawling halls'.

Marie Dubas, Lucienne Boyer.

Marie Dubas' stage personality was warm, passionate and volatile. Her remarkable versatility enabled her to switch, in the space of a minute from burlesque parody to something infinitely tender and lyrical. She was a unique combination of sorceress, clown and dreamer. 'As soon as the lights came on,' she said, 'it was the cue for satire. The target might be anyone, someone I'd passed in the street, a society woman, a snob, some cunning, seedy little woman, an adventuress, they were all grist to my mill. I satirized whatever was vulgar and comic in their lives. It was so amusing being vulgar like them and I used to enjoy myself . . .' Her first appearance was at the Olympia, and it was a song called *Pedro* that really made her.

Lucienne Boyer, with the famous contrast between her pale face and dark long-sleeved dress, also had a large following. She was tender, rather on the sad side, though when she sang a comic song, she showed she had an expressive face. It was she who introduced *Parlez-moi d'amour*.

Suzy Solidor.

Suzy Solidor, 'the girl with the flaxen hair', holds a unique record – the number of portraits made of her by famous painters. A blonde tigress with a baritone voice, she made her name around 1936–1937 with *Les filles de Saint-Malo*, and other sea-songs, also with *Mon légionnaire* and *Mon homme*.

Her act was both intimate and dramatic – a black piano covered with an orange shawl, a lamp, all other lights off, and a blonde singer – Suzy. She would lean against the piano, singing dreamy, sentimental songs of the period.

Charles Trenet, 'The Singing Madman'.

'*Je chante!*' cried Charles Trenet gaily in 1937, tossing his hat in the air and expressing man's everlasting need to sing. Maurice Chevalier, reviving his *Y a de la joie*, injected a boyish, lyrical note into the

Music-Hall that year. Trenet made his debut wearing a Chevalier-type straw hat, a pale blue suit, and on his posters, wings drawn by Cocteau and the nickname 'The Singing Madman'. He was one of those odd personalities, never satisfied, magnetic, full of regrets, frivolous, noble, with a gift for writing charming songs. Twenty years later, 'The Singing Madman' calmed down a bit, and after *Boum*, *La Mer* (adopted by the Japanese radio as its signature tune), *Train de nuit* and *La pluie*, he paid homage to French song in *Moi, j'aime le music-hall*. Almost all young contemporary singers owe a debt to his lyrical, imaginative, slightly surrealistic style. Trenet created his own world and drew it with comic and touching invention.

La Môme Piaf, the singing tragédienne.

Madame Piaf is the only real link between the pre-war and present-day generation of singers. Her powers of characterization, her strong, melodious voice, her surging, cracked timbre, her genius for transforming the sordid into song, have enabled her to break through the limits imposed on realistic singers like Yvonne George and Damia. It may seem inappropriate to mention 'realism' when referring to Edith Piaf, because she is in the tradition of François Villon and five centuries of popular song.

'I was born at five o'clock in the morning in 1915, out in the street, under a gas-lamp, with two policemen looking on . . .'
She had an eventful childhood . . .

She was first engaged by Louis Leplée at the Guernys, 54 rue Pierre Charron. It was Leplée who changed her name from Edith Gassion to Piaf, which is the name of a Paris sparrow. Maurice Chevalier was very struck by her. In 1931, she became headline news when her manager, the most famous cabaret manager in Paris, was murdered. She was suspected by the police, arrested, and then set free.
She then wrote the story of her childhood, *Mes Miracles*, which explains her remarkable personality.

It was Piaf who said that she couldn't live if she couldn't sing, that songs either get into her blood or leave her cold, Piaf who can't live without passion, without a real man, who sings *Hymne à l'amour*, who can't sleep, who lives by night, whose happiest moments are when the curtain rises, whose motto is 'To love'.

'Piaf stands for true quality. I've been fifty years in this profession and I've yet to meet her match,' said Maurice Chevalier. Piaf's love of her profession is shown in her preparation. She chooses her songs with immense care. Before selecting one, she may try a hundred. Once she has chosen, the real work begins – and the composer's nightmare. She may change words, even whole lines if they don't suit her. She worries away at a song, keeps singing it and making everyone listen. Quite often, she wakes up friends in the middle of the night to hum something over the telephone. She searches tirelessly to find the right gestures to go with a song. Not so long ago, in her vast, bare living-room in the boulevard Lannes, she was rehearsing twelve new songs. Two of the best were *Le boulevard du crime* and *Non, je ne regrette rien*.

The background to her songs is her own life – the life of the streets: Cosette of Belleville, a little girl going blind, the miracle of Sainte Thérèse de l'Enfant Jésus, the death of a baby, the flag of the Foreign Legion, and most famous of all, *La Vie en Rose*, which sold three million records.

The pioneers of song.

Before the large theatres won their international reputation, singing acts became popular in places that were part music-hall, part *café-concert*. In the early days, there was the Scala, the Parisiana, the Olympia, the Concert de la Poste, the Bateaux, the Concert-Mayol, quite apart from small local haunts like the Fourmi, the Fauvette and the Mésange.

Today, others have taken their place. The Concert Pacra still draws full houses. But apart from the Bobino, the Alhambra-Chevalier and various night-spots, cabarets like L'Echelle de Jacob, L'Ecluse and Le Bar Vert provide the necessary stamping-ground for young singers.

Damia and Fréhel are behind all modern songs. They began the revolt and prepared the way for Marianne Oswald. Marianne Oswald, in turn, prepared the way for Juliette Greco by singing songs by Prévert. But it took ten years and the success of *Les Feuilles Mortes* before things became easy. The pioneers must not be underestimated.

FORTUGÉ.   DRANEM.

MAYOL.   MONSIEUR PACRA.

BACH.

FERNANDEL « TOURLOUROU ». MARSEILLE. 1920.

70

POLAIRE. 1925.

1.

2.

1. PARISYS.

2. MAUD LOTTI.

3. SPINELLY (THÉATRE DES CAPUCINES).

4. VALESKA GERT. 1930.

5. MARIANNE OSWALD. 1935.

3.

4

5

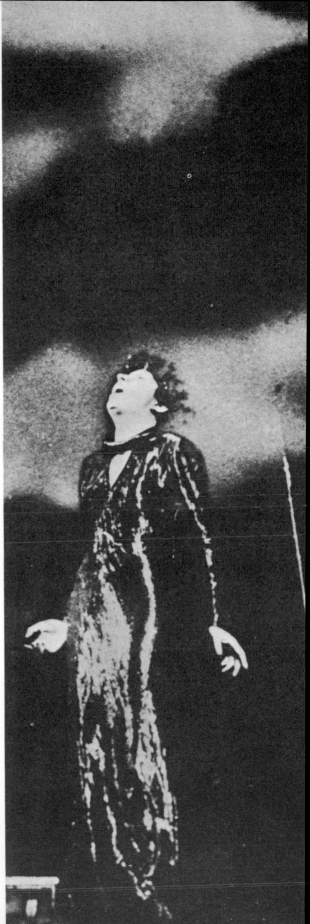

SOPHIE TUCKER. 1932.

MARIÈ DUBAS. 1930.

ARLETTY. REVUE DE RIP. 1934.

CHARPINI ET BRANCATO.

76

ÉDITH PIAF.

PALAIS DE JUSTICE. 1931.

ÉDITH PIAF. 1954.   CHARLES TRENET. 1938.

1

1. YVES MONTAND.
   EMPIRE. 1959.

2. ZIZI JEANMAIRE.
   ALHAMBRA. 1958.

3. JULIETTE GRÉCO.
   ROSE ROUGE. 1948.

2. 3.

MARLÈNE DIETRICH.
THÉATRE DE L'ÉTOILE. 196

Cécile Sorel

CASINO DE PARIS. 1934 ✶ P. 84. CÉCILE SOREL, HENRI VARNA (DIR.). CASINO DE PARIS. 1934.

Cécile Sorel at the Casino de Paris.

The happiest days of Mademoiselle Sorel's life were almost certainly during rehearsals at the Casino de Paris in December 1934. Her life had been full of struggles, vicissitudes and victories. Her action in leaving a national institution, the Comédie Française, and stooping to the Casino de Paris, was that of a woman who will stop at nothing.

Strength of character, courage, the will to improve, to scale new heights and taste every variety of theatrical fame, these were the qualities of this Lady Hamilton of the footlights. She had often, during her long waits between two performances at the Théâtre-Français, dreamed of the rowdy, colourful atmosphere of the Music-Hall.

This became clear on the night of her first show at the Casino when she appeared at the top of a golden staircase to one of the fullest houses ever seen in Paris. She was wearing a dress made of spirals of gold cloth, sparkling with tiny, bright, genuine diamonds. A long strip of velvet, neither a train nor a cloak, flowed out behind her on to the steps. A helmet, trimmed with plumes of every shade of red from flame to pink, crowned her warrior-like appearance.

The audience, as it watched her walking down 'her' staircase, seemed to witness the apotheosis of joy and happiness. She was no longer a woman, but a symbol. She didn't walk down, she seemed to gravitate. She was a world to herself, a fairy-tale world with all the divine trappings, and as she glided down down towards the footlights, the entire audience found itself rising to its feet . . .

St Germain-des-Prés and after

The Left-Bank style: Juliette Greco, Yves Montand.

CELLARS had already enjoyed a certain vogue, but it was about 1945 that the young people of St Germain-des-Prés acquired their habit of meeting in them (a habit which grew up during the war, possibly) and turning them into night clubs. The Tabou, so-called Existentialist cellar, was one of the best known, and one of the most famous music-hall singers began there – a high-priestess with the most tortured name in Spanish painting – Greco; but also the most romantic and delightful Christian name in Shakespeare – Juliette.

In the early days, this muse of Existentialism, as she was called, was very different from the sophisticated woman of today. On the plump side, with long dirty hair and an aquiline nose, she quickly learnt, through her own remarkable intuition (and the advice of Jean-Paul Sartre) how to choose really good songs. She revived some of Prévert's which Marianne Oswald had sung, recited poems by Desnos and Mauriac, and even sang bits of *The Threepenny Opera*. She worked unsparingly at her songs, improving her diction, which was, at first, indifferent, until she reached the high standards she had set herself. Films claimed her for a while, but they were not her best medium.

During the winter of 1960–61, she appeared at the Bobino in a new act. Though she still wore a long, black, close-fitting dress, the muse of the cellars had disappeared. It is common knowledge how carefully she chose her writers, and how poignantly and intelligently she interpreted them. She was even able to trace her own line of descent through Yvette Guilbert, Damia, Marianne Oswald and Agnès Capri. She may well yet surpass the last two. To their qualities she has added two rare gifts of her own: incisive humour and tender disillusion, which help her express the age she lives in . . . Juliette Greco's career, her great career, is just beginning . . .

After the Tabou and the Lorientais, which had a very good New Orleans band under Claude Luter, came the Rose Rouge, (which no longer exists) in the rue de Rennes. The Rose Rouge created a highly individual style of cabaret. This style, which had been pioneered by Agnès Capri during the war, consisted of what in the nineteenth century were called *proverbes*, a form of intimate theatre combining song, mime and dance. It also produced the Frères Jacques, whose costume – tight-fitting black jersey-cum-pointed waistcoat, top hat and white gloves – is famous the world over. In its early days, the Rose Rouge was directed by Yves Robert with the help of a remarkable team: Rosy Varte, Guy Pierault, Jean Marie Amato and Jacques Hilling. Among some of its best presentations were *Fantomas*, to the music of Kurt Weil, *Les Bonnes Manières* and Raymond Queneau's *exercises de style*.

Every night at the Rose Rouge, you could watch well-known actors and singers, such as Yves Montand who in the last few years has become the biggest French international name in Show Business. Obviously destined to take on the mantle of Chevalier, he is at the height of his career. In 1939, this Marseilles Italian gave up metallurgy at the age of sixteen to become a singer. He went to the Marseilles Odéon, then to Toulouse and Bordeaux. In 1944, he reached Paris, and after engagements at the A.B.C., the Européen, the Bobino and the Moulin-Rouge, he met and was advised by Edith Piaf. In 1945, he was top-of-the-bill at the Etoile. Since then, he has become a leading Hollywood star.

Brassens, Mouloudji.

George Brassens has described himself as '*le pornographe du phonographe*'. Though he plays the parts of ne'er-do-wells, grave-diggers and bad lots, he is, in fact, modest, solitary, even slightly irascible by nature. As a small boy, sitting on a classroom bench at the Collège de Sète – he was in with the dunces – he was already writing songs of incredible severity. He is the sort of man who is never really at ease, who needs to express himself and wear his heart on his sleeve. This amiable bear keeps himself to himself and lives with his cats (who keep turning up in his songs), his birds, his dogs and a friendly monkey. He claims to be 'a confirmed atheist', but God recurs in his mythology as often as his cats. According to Pierre Gascar, 'Brassens' art is linked with a medieval tradition which consisted of tossing into groups of people wallowing in pleasure and vanity and heedless of their fate, a stern reminder of the existence of God. Irony, comedy and self-derision may to some extent soften the rigour of a succinct but pitiless philosophy.'

Brassens, part François Villon, part Aristide Bruant-Montmartre *fin de siècle*, is one of the most humane of French singers. His theme is men, yet he shuns the noise and bustle of the city to wander in the fields, finding inspiration in the barrenest landscape. Slowly and tirelessly, he tramps the cornfields, hammering out a new song as he goes. He haunts this strange garden till nightfall, only to return again at sunrise.

The new songs he introduced at the Olympia in 1960, *L'Orage*, *Embrasse-les tous*, *Les funérailles d'antan*, were as successful as his old ones. Whether written four months or four years earlier, all had the freshness of works destined to live on.

Brassens and Mouloudji are the troubadours of French song. Mouloudji, Jewish and Arab by origin, is a kind of Berber, denizen of Pigalle night-life, rather grubby, rather gloomy, whose loves endure only in memories and regrets. A talented writer, he has published two books. One, a collection of mainly autobiographical short stories, reflects very much the same mood as his songs.

Gilbert Bécaud.

Gilbert Bécaud, *Monsieur cent mille volts*, dashes round the stage in every direction, yelling at his accompanist, dismantling his microphone, stamping his feet, flailing the air with his arms, literally 'possessed' and blasting the audience with his explosions. Maddening to some, fascinating to others, Bécaud is a real force of nature, endowed with first-class professional experience. The son of middle-class parents, he won a prize as a pianist at the Conservatoire de Nice, where his hero was Debussy. His immense success began when he met a civil servant with a passion for words, Louis Amade, who wrote *Les croix*. At the time, Bécaud was Jacques Pills' accompanist and quite unknown, but he learnt from Edith Piaf that a song has to be worked at like a book or a play. This young and attractive charmer quickly won the shopgirls' hearts, ousting Tino Rossi and Luis Mariano.

Charles Aznavour.

What made Charles Aznavour so appealing, with his hunched body, sloping shoulders, pale, emaciated face, and tired, cracked voice, was that he seemed to personify a race (he is Armenian) which had been hounded and persecuted down the centuries, a race of emigrants with carpet-bags, of families herded together in small tailors' shops in the rue des Blancs-Manteaux.

Today, at thirty-seven, he has become a great star. He has moved on, rejecting his old legend and exchanging it for a new one. Between himself and his audiences, he has interposed his screen heroes – heroes which are, incidentally, born victims, doomed to disaster. He probably appears to better advantage on the stage, where his songs have acquired a new musical quality without any loss of impact. Two marvellous new songs of his are *Je me voyais déjà* and *Tu te laissais aller*.

He is a kind of French Sinatra. Like Sinatra, he now lives surrounded by a bodyguard in boots and leather jackets, drives huge American cars and supports a battalion of mercenaries on his 'ranch' in the French countryside which he has transformed into a veritable fortress. At present, with his author's rights (most of the songs he sings are composed by himself), he must earn sixty million francs (about forty thousand pounds) a year.

The Reign of Hysteria: Rock 'n' Roll.

Singers come under this heading because, even if they are not actually mad themselves, they have the power to work their audiences, or at least a certain generation, into a state of wild hysteria.

Some young idols have earned themselves the right to be pushed around and have the buttons ripped off their coats by hysterical teen-age girls. Tino Rossi, before the war, Henri Garat, in the provinces, and a few others, had the same effect on their audiences. Seats have been smashed at the Olympia during concerts by Gilbert Bécaud, for instance, or by certain coloured musicians. It is surprising to learn that not all countries worship the same idols. Johnny Ray caused havoc at the London Palladium, but had little or no effect in Paris. At present, Paul Anka and Sacha Distel hold the record for disturbances in France.

The early days of rock 'n' roll provoked mass hysteria in Holland and Germany. Things were fairly calm in France, but rock 'n' roll has come to stay. All rhythm stars sing rock. Accordionists, selling thousands of records, have changed the old-style Saturday night dances beyond all recognition. More important, though, are the 'singing playboys', such as Richard Anthony and Johnny Hallyday. Others include Hugues Aufray, Jean Paul Vignon, Jean Beriac and Claude Pison.

Sacha Distel.

Sacha Distel is the latest 'playboy' of the world of song. He provokes riots wherever he goes in France and has to have police protection every night. His success has been phenomenal, the quickest rise to fame in the history of French song since Mistinguett and Chevalier. Girls in bobby-socks and boys in leather jackets and jeans besiege him in every town he visits, try to touch him, smother him with kisses or make off with a photo, autograph or souvenir button. He emerges from these passionate skirmishes, his hair rumpled and collar torn.

Every music-hall artist needs a song to start him off, a song which suddenly finds itself on everyone's lips. Mistinguett had *Mon homme:* Chevalier *Ma pomme.* Distel's was *Scoubidou.* This was the magic formula that has put him ahead of Bécaud, Brassens and Aznavour in the world of song. He got his first break from the massive publicity lavished on his affair with Brigitte Bardot, and since then has had to work hard to make his talent measure up to his fame. In less than a year, with a boyish grin and a silly song, he has scaled the dizzy heights of fame, to become the idol of French youth and the friend of every jazz-lover.

Zizi Jeanmaire, Colette Renard.

Zizi Jeanmaire was a ballet star who switched to a less classical style when she joined Roland Petit whom she later married. With him, she created the famous ballet *Carmen*, which toured the world. She went to Hollywood to act in musical comedy films, made *Daddy Longlegs* with Fred Astaire, and built up a singing act. About three or four years ago, an attempt was made to turn her into another Mistinguett, but her slight physique and lightweight personality were against her. Zizi, called 'La chatte' and 'La croqueuse de diamants', with her slightly raucous voice and Parisian cockney, is particularly good in *ballets chantants* and will always be sure of a following.

Colette Renard, the creator of *Irma La Douce*, is altogether different. Her songs are both vulgar and delightful; one, *Mon homme est un vrai guignol*, is a masterpiece. But her movements and gestures are often inept and awkward, and she is better heard than seen.

90

Marlene Dietrich.

On the 28th November 1959, in Paris, an audience of 1500 people held its breath as Marlene Dietrich came on stage for her first night at the Etoile. She sang for three-quarters of an hour, thrilled everyone and earned a thousand pounds a night. Her act was one of the best-planned ever seen. She rehearsed ten days non-stop, and not always in the friendliest of atmospheres. She even had the stalls moved back five rows, so that she could be seen from the back of the theatre properly lit.

She sang fourteen songs, the first few in a tight-fitting pink-and-diamond dress, over which she wore a huge swan-down wrap for her entrance. Then, in top-hat and tails, she sang five songs written for men. She would have liked to sing *La Vie en Rose*, but the song has become Edith Piaf's rightful property, and only Piaf may sing it in France.

Her German tour was not a success. Thirty years after the success of *The Blue Angel*, this daughter of an Uhlan officer had taken on a hard task. The Germans couldn't forgive her for having become Americanized, for having won the Legion of Honour, and for having marched in khaki down the Champs-Elysées after the war, behind the flag of the American Legion.

'Quite obviously,' wrote Cocteau, 'one can't introduce Marlene. All the same, we can welcome her and thank her for being what she is. It's rare when someone enters into legend, armed from head to foot, just like that. Marlene, like children playing at knights in armour, entered into legend on horseback astride a chair.

Those who were lucky enough to go and see her, and hadn't heard about her sitting astride the chair, and listened to her singing *Ich bin von Kopf bis Fuss auf Liebe eingestellt*, will remember how perfect she was.

Why was it that this perfection wasn't merely a dazzling display of sex-appeal? Because, if Marlene went in for strip-tease and went right through with it, as she does with everything, the essence of her personality would still remain – a heart of gold.

This bird of paradise, this bark in full spread of sail, this miracle of grace whose feathers, plumes and furs seem to become part of her own skin, is a rare force, a force of active goodness, prepared to cross oceans to do favours.

It would be idle to say more and abuse the honour she has done me in letting me talk to you about her. Better let her come on whose name begins with a caress and ends with a whiplash – Marlene . . . Dietrich.'

How better could one end? She has encompassed three decades of singers, always remaining true to herself, an example to the world of complete professionalism.

Opposite : IRWIN SISTERS. 'LES PAPILLONS FOLICHONS'. 1932.

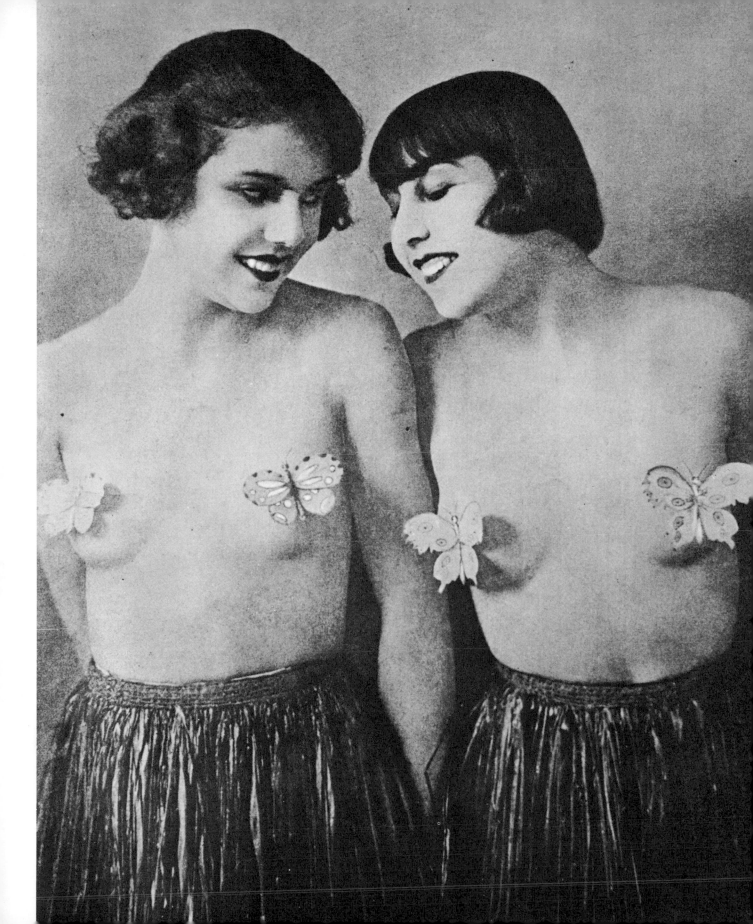

« LES PARISIENNES ».
CASTEL, DOREY SISTERS.

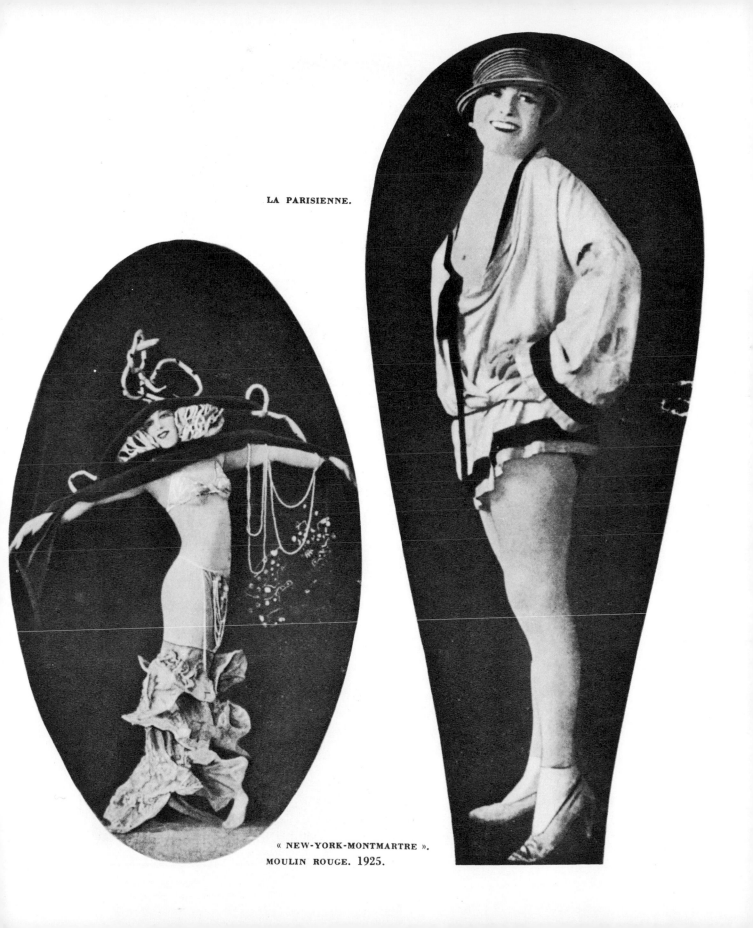

LA PARISIENNE.

« NEW-YORK-MONTMARTRE ».
MOULIN ROUGE. 1925.

« LA PRIÈRE ».
BALLET PLASTIQUE
ISSATCHENKO. 1932.

La Nicolska

1. MADEMOISELLE
   FLORIANE.
   « L'IDOLE DES INDES ».

2. « EVA »,
   « UN COUP DE FOLIE ».
   FOLIES BERGÈRE.
   COSTUME : PAUL SAL-
   TENHAMMER. 1930.

3. « RUSSIAN MONT-
   MARTRE ». MOULIN
   ROUGE. 1925.

1

2

3

« LES CHATTES ».

LA MOME MOINEAU. 1927.

« LES MESSES NOIRES » (THE BLACK MASS).

P. 104: Miss Harryet.
Concert Mayol. 1927.

The Paris Music-Halls

The Golden Age of the Casino de Paris.

THE MAD YEARS had arrived, years of *folie* in the Music-Hall,
beginning with the return of Gaby Deslys in 1917, continuing till about
1934 or 1935, and still lingering on today . . . All you need do is glance at a
programme at the Folies-Bergère, the Casino de Paris or the
Concert-Mayol.

Beretta and Volterra reopened the Olympia in October 1914.
Between 1915 and 1928, every big star, from Grock to Maurice
Chevalier, who made his come-back there on his return from being a
prisoner-of-war, played there.

After the Olympia, came the hey-day of the Casino de Paris under
Volterra, then under Dufrenne and Varna, and when Dufrenne died, under
Varna on his own. In 1917, Léon Volterra, after his quarrel with Beretta,
decided to take over this unwanted music-hall, and he opened it in 1917
with the revue *Laissez-les tomber*. The entire press sang the praises
both of Gaby Deslys and the revue itself, and the theatre was packed for
weeks and months. The revue which followed *Laissez-les tomber* was
christened *Boum* because its first night coincided with the first bombardment
of Paris by Big Bertha.

Pa-ri-ki-ri, in 1918, was the third big revue at the Casino.
It was the first of a long series, because both Mistinguett and Maurice
Chevalier made their debuts in it. 'Miss' was becoming very famous. She
had first appeared at the Eldorado in about 1900. Another name made by
Pa-ri-ki-ri was the designer, Gesmar. 'He was a young genius.
He worked on many shows and it was thanks to him as well as to Bakst,
a few years earlier, that the art of costume design developed so greatly.
Everyone called him "*Maman*", because he used to mother Mistinguett so
conscientiously, never leaving her side for a minute. He was seventeen.'

In *La Grande Revue* in 1919, Max Dearly headed the bill. It was the
last time that he and 'Miss' danced together and performed the
valse chaloupée . . .

Paris qui danse, in November 1919, was one of the most successful
revues. It owed its title to the grand finale, which featured dances that
had been fashionable down the ages, from the quadrilles of the Lautrec
period to the tangos, craze of the pre-1914 years, imported from the
Argentine by Professor Duc. It was the first revue in which a woman
appeared naked on a music-hall stage . . .

Then there were *Cache ton piano* and *Paris qui jazz* during the winter of 1920–21. The latter was without doubt the greatest of all the Casino de Paris revues, thanks to Maurice Yvain's *Mon homme*. It was also Poiret's first chance as a costume-designer and the sets were by José de Zamora. Between them they created two or three tableaux which set a new lavish fashion in music-hall décor.

Avec le sourire and *Dans un fauteuil* at the Casino saw the debuts of Saint-Granier and Marie Dubas, who hadn't then taken up singing, but danced and acted in sketches. *Paris en l'air* introduced Earl Leslie, who had danced for Cochran with the Dolly Sisters. It also featured Maurice Yvain's song *J'en ai marre*.

Then there was the *Revue des Etoiles* with Mitty and Tillio: two numbers were singled out for praise – the phantom ship and the desert scene, and the extremely beautiful finale. With *En douce* in 1923, after the fire, the Casino staged a sensational reopening, with a glass water-tank containing twenty thousand gallons of water, which rose magnificently from below stage by means of a lift. At the end of the show, the entire company dived into the tank. The next revue, also in 1923, *Y a qu'à Paris*, introduced Barbette. *On dit ça*, in the same year, had Jane Marnac and Captain Woodward's Performing Seals. Jenny Golder also made a big hit in it, and so did Edmonde Guy, dancing with Van Duren in a Spanish slum number . . . Van Duren, who committed suicide a few years later, had a great success in *La Revue Olympique*, in which Parisys also starred.

In 1925, the Hoffman Girls made their first appearance in the revue *New York-Montmartre*. The music was by Vincent Scotto, Maurice Yvain, Moretti, Padilla, Charles Laurent and Chantier, with costumes by Robert Piguet and Zamora.

The Folies-Bergère

The names of Folies-Bergère revues often rightly contained the word *folie*. In 1923, there was *En pleine folie*, and in 1925, *Un soir de folie*, with Nina Payne. (The Perpetual Adoration and chastity belt numbers were particularly successful and the famous Baron de Meyer came and took photographs of the company.) In 1927, Derval presented *Un vent de folie* and *Hyper-revue*, and in 1930, *Un coup de folie*, with Feral Benga, the negro dancer, Jackson and Le Nu Polisson. Among the chief sketches in *Un vent de folie* were *L'horloge des fêtes*, *Le vol des libellules*, *Plantation* with Joséphine Baker, *La galerie de Cléopâtre*, *La gondole du Doge*,

Sur un lit de roses, Le monde en prière and *Sous la tente d'Ali Baba*. In 1926–7, there was *La folie du jour*, with Chrysis, the Epp Sisters, Dorville, Castel, Alibert, Joséphine Baker, Pepa Bonafé, Maryse and Tymga. *L'usine de folie*, in 1931, was equally sensational: it also had Feral Benga, as well as Chrysis, the Epp Sisters, Alfred Jackson and Stan Randall . . . *Folies* upon *folies* . . .

    Coeurs en folie at the Folies-Bergère was, according to Monsieur Lemarchand, critic of the *Figaro*, writing in 1924, an evocation of 'the Napoleonic period from the Consulship to the Empire, the Directoire fashions on show only proving that *plus ça change, plus c'est la même chose* . . .

and the fête by night in the Tivoli Gardens was remarkably like present-day garden parties . . . There was a *mongolfière*, forerunner of the aeroplane . . . and to salute the triumph of might – highly topical – there were magnificent girls blowing into long trumpets, marching at the head of muscular boxers and armed athletes, portrayed by lithe and attractive girls. The superb reconstruction of a Roman chariot-race had only one fault – it was too short. There was a gleaming show-case in which young women in tasteful deshabillé represented rings, bracelets, ear-rings, pendants and clasps . . . Some scenes, apart from their visual splendour, were strikingly picturesque. Among the most successful was the Tarasque monster, with terrible eyes and wide-open mouth, belching smoke, all hundred feet of which suddenly dissolved into a graceful, well-trained troupe of dancers . . .

The final number was set in Egypt. On stage was a swimming-bath and, behind it, an ancient sphinx, surrounded by princesses. Skilful swimmers gave a display of graceful, flowing strokes, bringing the show to a fine artistic climax . . .

In 1929, the Folies-Bergère sub-titled their show *De la folie pure*, and so it was. It began with the Belle of Athens, went on to the Belle of Seville and the Belle of Moscow and the Belle of New York and the Belle of Vienna and ended up with the Belles of Paris.

Paris ville de joie, Paris ville de volupté was Derval's formula in *Un coup de folie* in 1930. Among the sketches were *Paris-Gaîté, Le Polichinelle de bébé, Le Polichinelle dans le tiroir, Une reine en folie, Catherine de Russie, Le ballet des faunes* (inspired by *L'après-midi d'un faune;* they decided that one faun was in-adequate, so they had several), *Les tableaux patriotiques de* 1918, and *Le nu naïf, Le Paris nudiste, Le nu polisson, Le nu des noces, Le nu mondain, Le nu exotique, Le nu lascif, Le nu érotique, Le nu sadique* and *Les sirènes de Ceylan* . . .

From the Moulin-Rouge to the Lido.

The 1925 Moulin-Rouge revue was sheer frenzy, with *Les messes noires, La tentation de Saint Antoine, Montmartre à la Russe, Le bain de Bilitis,*

and at the Ba-ta-clan, the Broquin Sisters wiggled their way through
La danse des libellules . . .

Later the revues at the Palace and other music-halls were equally
crazy: *Femmes et Sports* had Georges Carpentier, Florence Walton
and the Palace Beauties, a hotch-potch of mock-boxing and pretty girls.
Carpentier had to come on with Chrysis and the dancers and gymnasts,
and kick up a leg, and La Môme Moineau came on stage naked, in her
own inimitable way. Added to these were the mysterious Nadja in
gold lamé, golf at la Baule, Byzantine orgies, exotic dresses, luminous
aeroplanes and an ostrich farm; together with women boxers, so-called
flower battles, Gina Palerme, Parisys, Damia and Germaine Lix,
the Mayol Beauties in and out of swimming-pools, and a lady called
Betschoven.

Another revue, worthy of a poem by Prévert, was *Le luxe de Paris*.
It had Raquel Meller, the first buds of spring, a power-station made of
silk flowers, and in a welter of feathers and a mass of jewels, the fabulous
Irwin Sisters, and women disguised as ruby pendants, carrying the
inevitable parasols and endlessly dancing fox-trots, charlestons,
black-bottoms, fados and cake-walks. La Nicolska gave a 'modernistic'
nude dance called *mysteriom-biblique-et-la-naissance-de-la-lascivité-et-de-la*

110

passion. A new fashion was born – gaily-coloured umbrellas against a
Paris sky.

Of one Palace revue it was said: 'In this new revue, Oscar Dufrenne
and Varna have brought off a genuine artistic triumph, and the forty-five
numbers in *Vive la femme* have all their traditional splendour and good
taste.' Among these were *La voix des sirènes, A la mode de quand,
par nos grands couturiers: Poiret, Redfern, Lanvin, Drecoll, Patou et Worth,
La serre aux camélias, Le théâtre simultanéiste, Les chansons des chevaliers,
La cueillette des fleurs en Californie, Chili bom bom, Le divan des fumeuses,
La luxure, La danseuse Mercédès dans un sketch très chat . . . ié, La lune au
music-hall* and *Les papillons folichons.*

Also at the Palace were *Le luxe de Paris, Le luxe des bijoux* and
Pomiés, le music-hall en 80 danses . . .

The huge Théâtre des Champs-Elysées was converted, under the
direction of André Daven and Rolph de Maré, into a variety music-hall.
Various kinds of dancing were performed there, from Pavlova to Jean
Borlin, from the Swedish Ballet to Joséphine Baker with the *Revue Nègre.*
In 1925, the revue almost didn't go on. Everyone found the negroes did too
much tap-dancing, which became monotonous. The variety music-hall
was never a popular success: it was too chic.

ROSERAY ET CAPELLA. 1926.

1 MISS HAYES. 1930.

2. COCCINELLE, « TRAVES

CARROUSEL. 1957.

3. FERAL BENGA.

FOLIES BERGÈRE. 1931.

2   3

LE BAIN ROMAIN (THE ROMAN BATH). LIDO. 1957.
STOWITTS. FOLIES BERGÈRE. 1924.

NUS. NOUVELLE ÉVE. 1955

NEL. CASINO DE PARIS. 19

119 pour Mᵉ Marant.
lui but l'affaire
Nel Herrun
1927

119

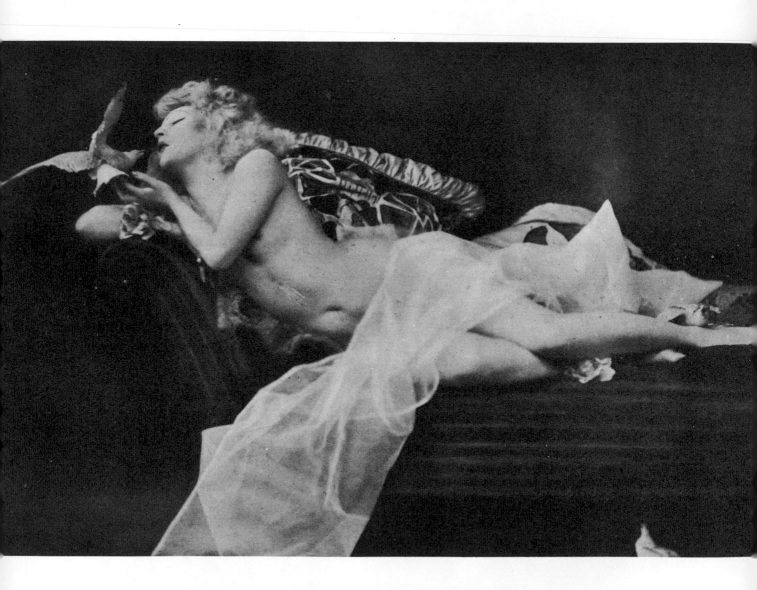

CHRYSIS. 1927.

FRÉDÉRIC REY. FOLIES BERGÈRE. 1950.

P. 122. L'USINE A FOLIES. FOLIES BERGÈRE. 1931.
P. 123 : FINAL. FOLIES BERGÈRE. 1958.

MARIANNE CONRAD, FLEMING. LIDO.

124

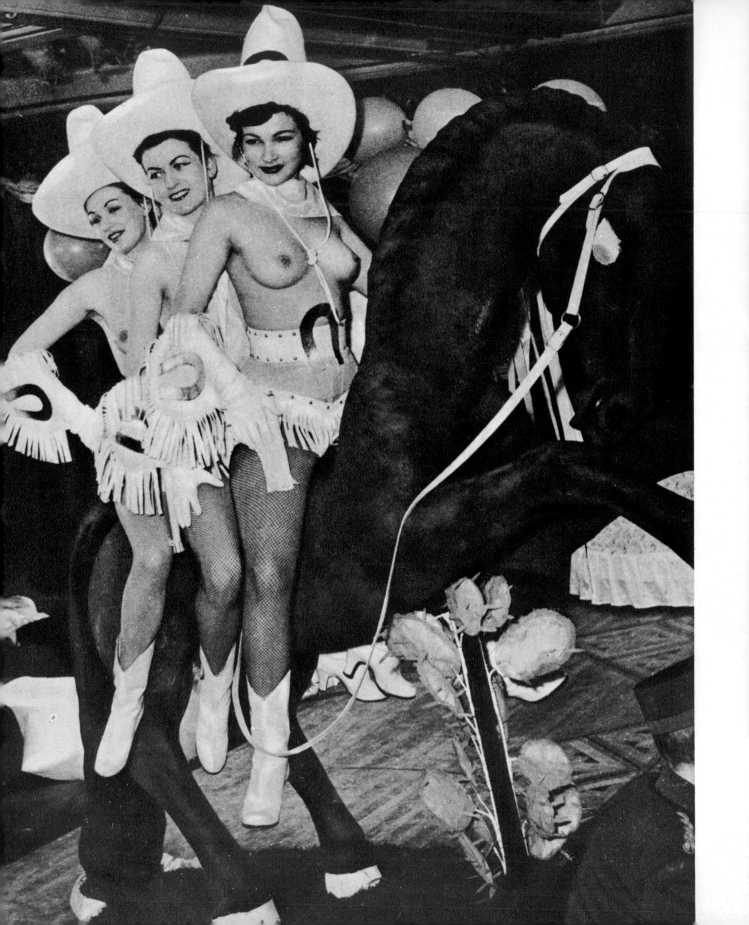

CARNAVAL EXOTIQUE. « VOILA ». LIDO. 1953.   SPADOLINI. 1937.

GEORGES REICH. BALLETS HO. OLYMPIA. 1959.

« LE BAIN ROMAIN ». LIDO.

« LEDA ». FOLIES BERGÈRE.

P. 132 : MICHEL BASSE. LIDO. 1954.

P. 133 : RHAPSODIE IN BLUE. LIDO.

BALLETS ALARIA. « PRESTIGE ». LIDO. 1957.

1. EDMONDE GUY.   2. MARIANNE CONRAD, FLEMING.

4. JENNY STEINER, ROBERTS.   3. CARPENTIER ET WALTON.

In 1924, the Société Pathé built the Empire, and its directors, Dufrenne and Varna, styled it 'Music-Hall-Circus'. They presented Chevalier, the Revellers, Jeannette MacDonald, Eleanora Duse, Raquel Meller, Frégoli, Jackie Coogan, Sophie Tucker, Carlos Grandel, Grock, Jack Hilton, and in the arena, the best circus-acts in the world, such as Orlando, Captain Wall and his Crocodiles, Princess Sabayana and her Sea-lions, etc. . . . In October 1931, they closed down. Stavinsky then took over the Empire and presented Hungarian operetta . . .

The Bobino, in the rue de la Gaîté, a street famous for its music-halls, was for a long time a local *café-concert* and cinema, then became a music-hall under the direction of Castille junior.

The Ba-ta-clan, on the boulevard Voltaire, saw Fragson's debut, Paulus, and Bruant with a revival of his famous cabaret; it was there that Colonel Cody, the celebrated Buffalo Bill, wounded his wife. Madame Rasimi took over the theatre again in 1910. Her most famous guest artist was Edmonde Guy. People still remember *Tin-tin premier*, a famous operetta-revue from *La danse des libellules*, based on music by Franz Lehar, which opened on the 15th March 1924, with Marie Dubas, Mario, Bever, the Broquin Sisters, with costumes by Madame Rasimi and sets by José de Zamora.

Thanks to Lord Baradsford, an English manager who bought the theatre, the Alhambra had a big success before the Great War: 'He presented the finest acts in the world, over which he had exclusive rights, being the only manager who could guarantee two years' continuous work, because of the many theatres he owned. Up till his tragic death, Fragson starred there twice a year. Gaby Deslys and Harry Pilcer appeared there, in a sketch about an accident, in which a motor-car was crushed by a train. Later on, Mistinguett featured another train, the one in *J'en ai marre*. Barbette appeared there on his first visit to Paris, and so did Lavigne, Chris Richards, and Joe Jackson, the bicycle tramp, Grock and Baggessen, and the finest tight-rope walkers, the mulatto Robeglio, the Codonas, Birdie Millman, Coleano, the very best musicians, in that typically English auditorium, all red plush and mahogany . . .'

Since the last war, revues have made little progress, and the only theatre which has kept up the tradition of high standards and lavishness is the Lido. Pierre-Louis Guérin and René Fraday have done much to ensure its continuing success. Paul Derval's Folies-Bergère and Henri Varna's Casino de Paris live off their past glories. The Concert-Mayol

has confined itself to strip-tease, the Alhambra – Maurice Chevalier, the Etoile and the Bobino only put on occasional revues. The Concert-Pacra has remained one of the few bastions of the old *café-concerts*, and old-fashioned singers perform alongside young talent – thanks to Madame Pacra. The Tabarin, which was once resplendent under Sandrini's direction, no longer exists. Pierre Louis Guérin's example, at the Lido, is one that must be followed, if the Music-Hall, with all its *folie* and glamour, is to be saved.

Stars and Specialities

Spanish Acts.

MANY PERFORMERS came from across the Pyrenees. In the early days, they arrived in their hundreds, with their shawls, combs, flounces, swaying hips, guitars, castanets, stamping their feet even more sharply and imperiously than the Americans . . . a hotch-potch of Carmen and Pepita, which reached a peak of frenzy, then died down. Only a few will be remembered: Isabelita Ruiz, Amparito Medina, and Argentina . . .

Argentina danced first at the Alhambra, then at the Empire and very quickly made herself a reputation. She was a tremendous success at the Opéra-Comique. She then ambitiously started Spanish Ballet, and grouped round her musicians, dancers, painters and poets, so that Paris could witness the artistic wealth of Spain in one huge show. It went on at the Théâtre Femina in 1928.

Argentina had a long haughty face and an unusually thin body. Her remarkable dancing talents put her streets ahead of all other rivals, including the members of her own troupe (with the possible exception of Lolita Las) whose cleverest dancers were merely virtuoso performers. Only Vincente Escudero, with his fine sense of rhythm and wonderful stillness, ever revealed a comparable talent.

The most recent Spanish rivals include Teresa and Luisillo, Rosario and Antonio, then Antonio on his own. Antonio is one of the greatest today. Too many of the others are merely talented folk-dancers.

Raquel Meller was planning a come-back not so very long ago. She is very old, very rich, and now lives very comfortably in Spain, where such artists are traditionally respected. She performed for the first time at the Olympia in 1920, but was first noticed in 1928. For years she was tremendously successful in Spain and at the Arnao Theatre in Barcelona where she made both her first and her last appearances. She had exquisite looks: delicate features, dark, gentle eyes, a beautiful mouth and soft voice. Raquel Meller became the idol of Paris. There were pictures of her everywhere, and her songs were widely sung, especially *El Relicario* and *La Violettera*, those little 'masterpieces' by Padilla. Some still remember the delightful way she used to offer violets to her adoring audiences, murmuring in her soft voice: '*Beaux senors et senoritas . . .*'

At one time, Spanish acts were so popular, that German dancers like Harry First dressed up as Castilians. Others, both past and present, who deserve mention, include Carmen Amaya, Amalia Rodriguez (Portuguese), Pilar Lopez, Espanita Cortez, and Tina Meller.

Sisters, Brothers and Girls.

There was yet another invasion – this time by the Schwartz, Irwin, Dolly and Guy Sisters, the Rocky Twins and many others . . .

The art of well-drilled, vigorous dancing can be practised by very small troupes, and even a single pair of dancers can be very effective. The Dolly Sisters achieved a remarkable and entirely deserved success in this way. They transformed the well-established charleston into a new dance – 'the dirty pig'. They also set a new fashion in make-up: shaded eye-lids, round, pink cheeks, Cupid's bow lips, and short hair, with a fringe covering the forehead. In 1926, the Hoffman Girls appeared in Paris for the first time in the revue *New York-Montmartre:* the Bluebell Girls of today are their modern counterparts.

The Hoffman Girls' revue was far more streamlined than all previous ones. It wasn't weighted down with a lot of long-drawn-out, not very funny sketches. There was no claque slavishly insisting on encores. No one came back on stage again for a bow. As soon as one number was over, the next began, a technique derived from the cinema.

'One number, *Webbing*, featured eighteen girls in white-diamond-studded sweaters, hanging by their wrists and teeth from long white cords over the audience's heads . . .'

Jugglers.

Everyone ought to have seen Enrico Rastelli at least once in his
life. Rastelli was a study in elegance and perfection. No one could resist the
sight of him in his trunks, white stockings, pumps and a kind of loose
smock. His natural grace, enhanced by his remarkable skill, was one of the
secrets of his success, though almost certainly the least important, and only
a kind of additional flourish to a very long act in which he exhausted
all the possibilities of juggling: with balls, asymmetrical juggling (in which
his hands and feet made objects move in opposite directions), acrobatic
stunts, with jumps and leaps an integral part of the juggling, and last and
best of all, the game of rods, a very old game of Japanese origin, which
Rastelli revived in a series of extraordinary variations. A technical
description could not possibly do justice to the richness and variety of his
act. 'If you said that the balls seemed to have been "tamed" as they
climbed Rastelli, bounced off his feet, or rested on his forehead,
like birds on a bird-fancier, you'd still be miles from the truth,' wrote
Pierrei Bost.
    Rastelli, whose father and grandfather were also jugglers,
was born in Italy in 1896. From 1912 to 1922, he remained in Russia, in
spite of the revolution, perfecting his act. He first achieved world fame at
the New York Hippodrome on the 18th November 1923, after which he
toured the world.
    He used to rehearse his tricks six or eight hours a day, and according to
Nico Rost, 'Rastelli became finally convinced that the technique of
juggling, as he knew it, was one of the most important forms of
human activity.'
    Mention should also be made of Rich Hayes, Paolo and also
Little John who, in spite of his youth, is amazingly skilful, and finally,
the 'divine' Rudy Cardenas.

Black bottoms, tangos and other dances.

We borrowed from the negroes the dance of 'the muddy
depths of the river'. This is the true origin of 'black bottom'.
    Billy Rearden and his partner, Mary Hay, danced the black bottom
with great success in 1927. But coloured dancers like the radiant
Florence Milles, and Johnny Higgins, had been the rage since the
Revue Nègre in 1926. The Moulin-Rouge presented the Blackbirds,

and the Théâtre de la Porte Saint-Martin, the Black-flowers.

Hal Sherman was the king of eccentric dancers. His great year was 1930: he had amazing facility, great powers of invention and danced with lazy ease.

Pomiès danced very well, her witty style, flair for mimicry and technical skill combined to make an excellent act.

Nina Payne was billed as 'the futurist and cubist dancer' and appeared at the Théâtre des Champs-Elysées after Loïe Fuller's *Ballets Fantastiques*.

Round about 1930, acrobatic dancing was stripped to its essentials. Men and women appeared practically naked: for instance, Brieux, Cariatys, Chrysis, Roseray and Capella. Classical dancers went over to the Music-Hall: Anton Dolin, Alicia Markova, Lisa Duncan, Gerlys and Lisia and many others. Viviane Romance, Jane Marnac and Irene Hilda began their careers as dancers. It should be noted that Mata-Hari, from about 1914, was already performing dances of a very daring nature. She was called 'the red dancer' or 'the magic ballerina'.

An exotic attraction was provided by Mademoiselle Sapotille, the idol of Arabia. Rumbas, beguines and congas from the West Indies all had their vogues. For about fifteen years, there have been numerous exotic ballets in Paris: Msinalini Sarabai's Hindu Ballet, Ram Gopal, Carmen Amaya's Gipsy Ballet, the Georgian Ballet, the Ballets Nègres and Nyota Inyoka's Ballet. Two of them broke box-office records: Katherine Dunham's Ballet and the Latin American Ballet. *Plus ça change, plus c'est la même chose* . . . the *Revue Japonaise* moved into the Moulin-Rouge with sets that would have delighted Toulouse-Lautrec, and the Olympia recently booked the *Nouvelle Revue Nègre*.

Another dancer, Edward Fleming, handsome and mysterious, with outstanding grace and talent, comes from Denmark and is the rightful successor to Harry Pilcer, Earl Leslie,

van Duren, Spadolini (the male nude) and Alperoff, that handful of dancers who won fame in the company of the fabulous Gaby Deslys, Jenny Golder, Edmonde Guy, Parisys, Spinelly and Mistinguett.

Two dancers had very similar careers: Georges Carpentier, after his boxing triumphs, appeared on the stage, and more recently, Sugar Ray Robinson took up tap-dancing.

Two more young dancers, of the 'sexy' variety, are still active: Alfredo Alaria, who went from the Casino de Paris to the Lido, and Georges Reich, Director of the Ballets Ho and a choreographer.

Illusionists.

Magicians are traditionally mysterious or foreign: they must wear Chinese or Hindu silk costumes. If they wear suits, they must have cloaks. Their décor must be elaborate, exotic or frightening. As dealers in miracles, everything they do must be wonderful and their audiences must be overwhelmed by their splendour and magic.

This magic has its origins in the world of fairy-tale. The wizard must enter with a confident flourish, carrying case, stick and hat, then his tie must suddenly change colour, his buttonhole start whizzing round on its stalk, and his case, stick and hat grow mysteriously longer . . .

Chinese magicians enjoyed a tremendous vogue. Among the greatest were Maskelyne, Benevol, de Bierre, de Ryss, Horace Goldin, de Steens, Canterelli and Le Grand Robert.

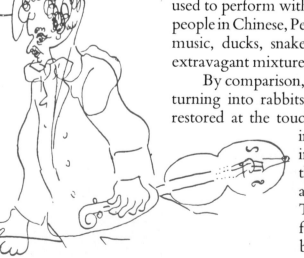

One remarkable conjurer, 'the Great Carmo', used to perform with a sumptuous entourage of thirty people in Chinese, Persian and Hindu costumes, dances, music, ducks, snakes, an elephant and a tiger – an extravagant mixture which delighted his audiences . . .

By comparison, run-of-the-mill tricks like scarves turning into rabbits, handkerchiefs being burnt and restored at the touch of a wand, watches vanishing into cones of paper, people appearing and disappearing mysteriously, the spiriting-away of a bird-cage and bird, are mere child's-play. The Indian rope-trick is out of fashion and fakirs are dying of broken hearts . . .

Female Impersonators, Rubber Men and a Contortionist.

    The best known female impersonator in France today is Coccinelle,
star of a specialized cabaret in the rue du Colisée. Coccinelle sings,
or rather, hums. He really seems to become a woman, with a woman's
figure, more insidiously feminine than the other, real girls. There are
many similar acts, of a more grotesque kind, though curiously effective,
such as Gaby de Montreal, Nana de Montparnasse, or Zambelli
with his Marlene Dietrich make-up. None is in the class of Barbette who
was, apart from anything else, an artist, a first-rate trapezist whose

disguise merely added piquancy to his act. Most of the rest are freaks, abnormal creatures, fit only to be shown at fair-grounds and stared at in a mixture of wonder, apprehension and pity. Little Tich, Charpini and Odett had brought skill and comedy to the art of female impersonation, but now these are mostly freaks of nature, hermaphrodites, exhibits from medical museums, to satisfy the public craving for monstrosity and perversion.

. . . Against a weird backcloth and in garish lighting a man's body slithers with nonchalant ease over the upright back of a chair. Then it slips effortlessly into a tea-chest. The lid is hastily clapped on and the audience swears there must be some trick in it. Obviously the tea-chest isn't that small, but it's small enough compared with the giant doubled up inside it . . . Chester Kingston combined the qualities of frog-man, snake-man and rubber-man, and in this way, was able to bring off some terrifying effects.

He was a human enigma, a strange phenomenon. Off-stage he was an elegantly-dressed young man, with a sensitive face and a lively mind. He appeared first at the Olympia, then at the Folies-Bergère, the Nouveau-Cirque, the Salle Marivaux, and from time to time at other Paris theatres.

Others in this rapidly-decreasing group of male and female contortionists include Mademoiselle Athéa, Miss Laurie de Wine, and Zaru, who performed in Paris up till 1957–8, and then disappeared without trace.

Eccentrics, Mutes and Raconteurs.

The attack, energy, fluency or silent eloquence of raconteurs, patter-merchants, street-vendors or mimes, never fails to delight audiences. Grock, Little Tich, Fernand Raynaud, Robert Lamoureux, Francis Blanche, Poiret and Serrault, Robert Dhéry, Christian Duvaleix, Roger Pierre and Jean-Marc Thibault, Philippe Noiret and Jean-Pierre Darras all had their triumphs.

Little Tich, who was more of a clown and a comedian than Grock, was one of the great figures in the early days of Music-Hall. His long-soled shoes, one of his cleverest inventions, enabled him to bend over and almost touch the ground. Charlie Chaplin was influenced by him. Pieral, another dwarf, dressed up, like Little Tich, as a prima donna or Spanish dancer. Joe Jackson, like Little Tich, used to appear on stage alone, using objects as partners. He was also a skilled acrobat.

144

« CŒURS EN FOLIE ». FOLIES BERGÈRE. 1924.

RAQUEL MELLER. 1929.

CARMEN VALENCIA. 1927.

146

AMALIA RODRIGUES. 1959.

ARGENTINA. 1930.

147

SISTERS.

1. LES SŒURS BROQUIN.
2. DODGE SISTERS.
3. RYAN AND BURKE.
4. DOLLY SISTERS.

1

2

3

150

LES SŒURS GUY.

152

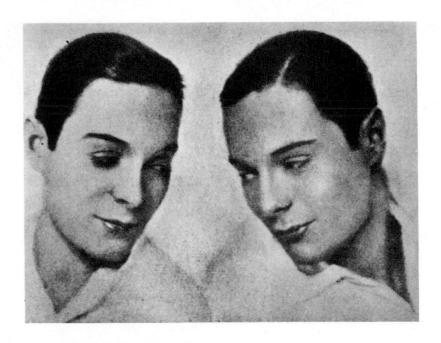

THE ROCKY TWINS.

THE PETER SISTERS. OLYMPIA. 1958.

LES FRÈRES JACQUES.

CIRCUS PARADE.
MADAME FANNY. 1930.

P. 156
LES SŒURS KESSLER
(BLUE BELLS). LIDO.

LES POPPESCU. 1922.
LES ALEX. 1917.

158

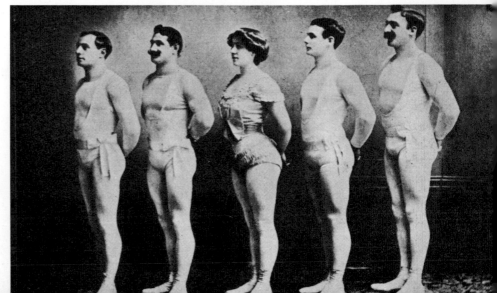

LES CODONA. 1925.

SILVAS JUNIORS. 1924.

SCÈNE DE CIRQUE. TABARIN. 1936.   GABY MARCÈS. 1933.

1

1. ZARU. 1957.

2-3. CHESTER KINSTON. 1925.

2

3

LES ATHENA (ART ET FORCE). 1923.

P. 166 : 1. PILOU AND PARTNER.

2. TAY-RU.

P. 167 : LITTLE JOHN. LIDO. 1957.

1   2

P. 168. BOGDI BROTHERS. LIDO.1956.

P. 169. LES FREDIANI. EMPIRE. 1957.

P. 170. MEDINA. SPECTACLE CASSANDRE. EMPIRE. 1954.

RASTELLI. 1922.

PAOLO. 1940.

REVERHOS. EMPIRE. 195

FELOVIS. 1924.

CARL BAGGESSEN. 1923.

174

DALDER, VENTRILOQUE.
1923.

ANDREU, RIVELS. 1924.

CLOWNS NAINS (ITALIA).

176

1916.

LITTLE TICH. 1923.

ANTONET. 1921.

JEAN FAZIL. 1924.

179

POMIÈS. 1924.

GILLES MARGARITIS (LES CHESTERFIELD). 1935.

LES BERNARD'S. LIDO. 1958.

GIRLS REVUE DU LIDO EMPIRE 1957

Gilles Margaritis had an excellent act of a similar kind with Roger Caccia before the war – the Chesterfields. This preceded the Chesterfolies, which they put on at the A.B.C. during the Occupation:

'The first time I saw them', wrote André Gide to Roger Martin du Gard on the 19th November 1938, 'this "musician" came on stage. He was rather hopeless, but pretty conceited and tragically infatuated with his "great art", and a tragic struggle developed between his "great art" (of the sublimest kind) and the disastrous inadequacy of his means of expression. His companion was a pleasant fellow, the sort of person who doesn't worry, who doesn't get involved in the tragedy, so the "great artist" shot him some disapproving looks. The disapproving looks continued but didn't make very much impression . . . I seem to remember that two years ago, the disasters occurred more slowly and only when the act was well under way. Possibly they decided to cut out anything which didn't appeal to the vast cosmopolitan audiences they had to please. However, I do remember that in that very ordinary cinema where I saw them for the first time, everything came across, even (to my surprise) the subtlest effects, and the show appealed to both the common man and the connoisseur. Nowadays, it seems to be aimed only at the common man. I still laugh, and applaud heartily, but something is missing . . .'

Robert Dhéry's burlesque revues *Branquignol, Dugudu, Ah les belles bacchantes!* and *La plume de ma tante*, which was a great success in London and later in New York, carried on in the Chesterfolies tradition which was itself inspired by the crazy humour of the Marx brothers and *Hellzapoppin'*, laced with a dash of French gaiety. Dhéry's shows had a pleasant, easy-going atmosphere, thanks to a young and engaging company which included Colette Brosset, Christian Duvaleix, a kind of hysterically funny Buster Keaton, Jean Carmet, who only had to walk down to the footlights and give his phoney 'knowing' look to make the audience laugh, the nervous and voluble de Funès, Rosine Luguet (daughter of André), Jacques Emmanuel, Gérard Calvi, the one-man orchestra, etc.

Henri Salvador should have been included among the singers, but he is primarily an eccentric comedian. So is Georges Ulmer, whose show was highly successful. So was Fernand Raynaud's, at the Variétés, with his imitations of Charlie Chaplin. Gérard Séty has an international reputation: his quick-change act, now a rare speciality act, is remarkable. He never fails to make an impression, but unfortunately his over-long if amusing script tends to become wearisome.

In the palmy days of the Music-Hall, Jean Richepin, then an old man, used to clamber up the stairs at the Olympia to the acrobats' dressing-rooms. The occupants, poor, simple, muscular and naked as the day they were born, were somewhat alarmed as Paul Franck introduced the old gentleman as 'a fellow-struggler from the French Academy'. Colette often used to be seen in the stuffy little bee-hives which sprawled on to the stage and were kept for famous women singers and the purveyors of boleros and fandangos: la Argentina, Laura de Santelmo, Isabelita Ruiz and many others.

Maurice Maeterlinck never failed to look in at the Olympia whenever he was in Paris. Rosemonde Gérard, Maurice Rostand and Rachilde adored the place. Young poets began their careers there. Henri Jeanson, who started the review *L'Entr'acte* at the age of twenty-one, was the *enfant terrible* of music-hall criticism.

L'Entr'acte, one of the most sensational reviews ever devoted to the circus and Music-Hall, first appeared in December 1925. René Bizet, writing in it, claimed that Music-Hall could save the theatre. Grock, the Dolly Sisters, Henri Duvernois, Legrand-Chabrier and Pierre Lazareff were among its contributors.

Night-clubs still put on fabulous shows. There will always be performers to provide the magic that the public wants. Kill-joys and pessimists may claim that the Music-Hall is not what it was: in a sense, this may be true, but the Music-Hall is far from dead. It may not be at its best and most brilliant in its present form, but it has many qualities. It supplies what men in every age have needed – magic.

The fact remains that if the links between the various acts sometimes lack style and intelligence, the actual framework of the shows, that is the technique of the acrobats, jugglers, dancers and singers has not declined; in fact, taking Rastelli as a yard-stick, it has progressed.

. . . The curtain, the huge red curtain is at last brought down, the audience leaves the theatre, its dream-world, and files out into the cold, dark street. Inside the theatre, perspiring men, boys and girls undress, take off their make-up, and five or ten minutes later, they too will be out in the street with the moving crowds. The lights, the splendour is over for them, too. Another day will pass, as they long for the few moments that will bring it all back again . . .

All that remains now is to thank these performers sincerely and profusely. Each of them has striven to present, in his own particular way, our day-dreams of beauty and unreality, offering us a fantasy-world that we have been glad to accept. Far, far less glorious than stage or screen actors, they pass by almost unnoticed, unrecognized in the streets. Their audiences ignore them, as they ignore many of the subtleties in their performances. Every second of an act represents months of work by a trapeze-artist or acrobat.

Remember the skill in mimicry of the clowns, remember the cyclists and the skaters. Remember the acrobats in pyramid-formation, or the gymnasts doing their head-stands and hand-stands, remember the Japanese tight-rope walkers. Remember the human ladders, the ventriloquists, the protean men, the beast-men, the monsters and the freaks . . .

Bibliography

LES MÉMOIRES DE JOSÉPHINE BAKER
Collected by Marcel Sauvage. Kra. 1927.

FOLIES-BERGÈRE
Paul Derval. Éditions de Paris. 1954.

LE CIRQUE ET LE MUSIC-HALL
Pierre Bost. Illus. Annenkov. Au sans Pareil. 1931.

CENT ANS DE MUSIC-HALL
Jacques-Charles. Éditions Jeheber. 1956.

HISTOIRE DU MUSIC-HALL
by L'Académie du Cirque et du Music-Hall. Illus. by Serge. Éditions
de Paris. 1954.

LES AMUSEURS DE PARIS
Maurice Verne. Éditions de France. 1932.

MUSÉES DE VOLUPTÉ
Maurice Verne. Éditions des Portiques.

LES USINES DU PLAISIR
Maurice Verne. Éditions des Portiques. 1930.

MA ROUTE ET MES CHANSONS
Maurice Chevalier. Julliard. 1948.

L'ENVERS DU MUSIC-HALL
Colette, of the Académie Goncourt. Flammarion. 1913.

LES ILLUSIONISTES ET LEURS SECRETS
Michel Seldow. Illus. Ray Bret-Koch. Fayard. 1959.

AU MUSIC-HALL
Gustave Fréjaville. Éditions du Nouveau-Monde. 1922.

CLOWNS, GIRLS, CINEMA
Dessins de Serge. 1928.

L'ÉPOQUE DU MUSIC-HALL
René Bizet. Éditions du Capitole. 1929.

LE MUSIC-HALL ET SES FIGURES
Louis-Léon Martin. Éditions de France. 1928.

MUSIC-HALL
Louis Roubaud. Querelle. 1929.

DE GABY DESLYS A MISTINGUETT
Jacques-Charles. Gallimard.

DE DRANEM A MAURICE CHEVALIER
    Jacques–Charles. Fayard.
LA VIE PRODIGIEUSE DE MAX DEARLY
    Jacques–Charles. Beziat.
MAURICE CHEVALIER, DE MENILMONTANT AU CASINO DE PARIS
    Rivollet. Grasset. 1927.
DU CAFÉ-CONCERT AU THÉATRE CHANTANT
    Lejay. Labbé. 1928.
DE GEORGIUS
BURLESQUE
    (An underground history of burlesque days.) New York. 1931.

Acknowledgements

THE AUTHOR is particularly grateful to Madame Gustave Fréjaville for the help she gave him in showing him her collection, also to Mesdames Bourgeois and Pacra, and Messieurs Pierre Barlatier, Pierre Demagny, Erté, Henri Varna, and Jose de Zamora, who were good enough to loan him precious documents.

Numerous quotations have been made from the writings of Maurice Verne, Pierre Bost, Gustave Fréjaville and Jacques-Charles.

Apart from the author's private researches, a great deal of material for this book has been supplied by Jacques-Charles, author of *Cent Ans de Music-Hall*.

The photographs in this work are by
DANIEL FRASNAY (for the more recent shows)
and also by the following agencies and photographers:
APERS, DE CORDON, HARCOURT, HARLINGUE, HONINGEN
HYNE, IRIS, LENI ISELIN, LELOIR, MARANT, MAYWALD, NOGRADY,
PIAZ, PIC, RAPHO and VIOLLET.

Photographic reproductions by
ETIENNE HUBERT.

French Editor
GILLES QUÉANT.